DESIGN AND TECHNOLOGY

Curriculum **B***ank*

KEY STAGE ONE
SCOTTISH LEVELS A-B

DESIGN AND TECHNOLOGY

CLARE BENSON

Published by Scholastic Ltd,
Villiers House,
Clarendon Avenue,
Leamington Spa,
Warwickshire CV32 5PR
Text © Clare Benson
© 1997 Scholastic Ltd
5 6 7 8 9 0   1 2 3 4 5 6

AUTHOR
CLARE BENSON

EDITOR
JOEL LANE

SERIES DESIGNER
LYNNE JOESBURY

DESIGNERS
TOBY LONG, MICKY PLEDGE AND ANNA OLIWA

ILLUSTRATIONS
NICK DIGGORY

COVER ILLUSTRATION
GAY STURROCK

INFORMATION TECHNOLOGY CONSULTANT
MARTIN BLOWS

SCOTTISH 5–14 LINKS
MARGARET SCOTT AND SUSAN GOW

Designed using Aldus Pagemaker

British Library Cataloguing-in-Publication Data
A catalogue record for this book is available from the
British Library.

ISBN 0-590-53404-1

Contents

DESIGN AND
TECHNOLOGY

Introduction

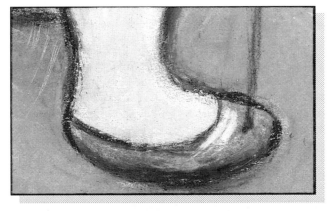

Scholastic Curriculum Bank is a series for all primary teachers, providing an essential planning tool for devising comprehensive schemes of work as well as an easily accessible and varied bank of practical, classroom-tested activities with photocopiable resources.

Designed to help planning for and implementation of progression, differentiation and assessment, *Scholastic Curriculum Bank* offers a structured range of stimulating activities with clearly stated learning objectives that reflect the programmes of study, and detailed lesson plans that allow busy teachers to put ideas into practice with the minimum amount of preparation time. The photocopiable sheets that accompany many of the activities provide ways of integrating purposeful application of knowledge and skills, differentiation, assessment and record-keeping.

Opportunities for formative assessment are highlighted within the activities where appropriate, while the 'Design and make assignments' in chapter 9 can be used for summative assessment. Ways of using information technology for different purposes and in different contexts, as a tool for communicating and handling information and as a means of investigating, are integrated into the activities where appropriate, and more explicit guidance is provided at the end of the book.

The series covers all the primary curriculum subjects, with separate books for Key Stages 1 and 2 or Scottish Levels A–B and C–E. It can be used as a flexible resource with any scheme, to fulfil National Curriculum and Scottish 5–14 requirements and to provide children with a variety of different learning experiences that will lead to effective acquisition of skills and knowledge.

DESIGN AND TECHNOLOGY

SCHOLASTIC CURRICULUM BANK DESIGN AND TECHNOLOGY

The Scholastic Curriculum Bank *Design and Technology* books help teachers to plan comprehensive and structured coverage of the programmes of study for this subject, and help pupils to develop the required skills and understanding through activities that promote design and technology capability. The primary curriculum for design and technology is covered in two books: one for each key stage. The Key Stage 2 book builds on the skills, knowledge and understanding which have been developed at Key Stage 1.

Bank of activities

This book provides a bank of activities that can be used in many different ways: to form the framework for a scheme of work; to add breadth, variety or extension to a core scheme; to support a cross-curricular topic; or as discrete tasks to help address particular learning needs.

Range

The range of activities provided will enable children to develop both their process skills and their practical skills, and their knowledge and understanding of structures, mechanisms, products and their application and health and safety. Opportunities for use of all the main areas of IT are highlighted throughout.

Communication skills

The activities develop technical vocabulary, language and communication skills by encouraging children to:
▲ use technical terms, diagrams and symbols;
▲ describe and discuss their work and respond to questioning;
▲ present their work using writing, quality products and a variety of drawing and modelling techniques.

Lesson plans

Detailed lesson plans, under clear headings, are given for each activity. They are set out in a standard way, so that the material is easy to follow and can be implemented readily in the classroom. The structure for each activity is as follows.

Activity title box

The information in the title box at the beginning of each activity, outlines the following key aspects:
▲ *Activity title and learning objective.* Each activity has a clearly stated learning objective, given in bold italics. These learning objectives break down aspects of the programmes of study into manageable teaching and learning units, and their purpose is to aid planning for breadth and balance. They can easily be referenced to the National Curriculum and Scottish 5–14 requirements by using the overview grids at the end of this chapter (pages 9 to 12).
▲ *Class organisation/likely duration.* Icons ♰♰ and ⏱ signpost the suggested group sizes for each activity and the approximate amount of time required to complete it. Small groups will generally mean up to four to six children, whereas larger groups could be ten to twelve children or even half a class. Timing arrangements are by their nature arbitrary, as so many factors are involved (including the children's previous skills and knowledge). However, it is important that the children be aware that there are constraints on the amount of time available – just as in the 'real world' of designers, manufacturers and producers.
▲ *Health and safety.* Where necessary, health and safety considerations are flagged by the icon ⚠. However, it is essential that checks be made as to what LEA regulations are in place. Further guidance can be obtained from the booklets *Make it Safe: Safety guidance for the teaching of Design and Technology at Key Stages 1 and 2* (National Association of Advisers and Inspectors in Design and Technology or NAAIDT) and *Be Safe!* (Association for Science Education or ASE).

Previous skills/knowledge needed

The information given here alerts teachers to particular knowledge or skills that the children will need prior to carrying out the activity.

Key background information

The information in this section is intended to set the scene and provide helpful guidance for the teacher. The guidance may relate to children's learning, to teachers' knowledge of design and technology or to both.

Language to be introduced

This section contains key words which

should be introduced to the children at some point during the activity. This can be achieved in a variety of ways: by producing a word bank at the start of the activity; by introducing each word in context and creating a word bank as the children progress through a task; or by introducing the words and making a word bank at the end of the task, to reinforce learning.

Preparation
Advice is given for those occasions where it is necessary for the teacher to prepare the children for the activity or to collect and prepare materials ahead of time.

Resources needed
All the equipment, materials and photocopiable sheets needed to carry out the activity are listed here, so that the children or the teacher can gather them together easily before the beginning of the teaching session. In the design and make assignments (DMA) section, 'typical resources' are indicated, since the children have to have the opportunity to choose some of the resources they will work with.

What to do
Easy-to-follow, step-by-step instructions are given for carrying out the activity, including (where appropriate) suggested points for discussion. Issues of classroom management are raised where relevant.

Suggestion(s) for extension/support
Where possible, ways of providing for easy differentiation are suggested. Thus the activities can be modified for less able pupils and extended for the more able.

Assessment opportunities
Each investigate, disassemble and evaluate activity (IDEA) and focused practical task (FPT) has clearly-staged assessment opportunities which relate directly to the learning objectives for that activity and provide the framework for ongoing assessment. By taking advantage of these assessment opportunities, teachers can be reassured that the stated learning objectives have been covered. Where appropriate, suitable questions for eliciting information from pupils are also included.

Opportunities for IT
Where opportunities for IT application arise, these are briefly outlined with reference to particularly suitable types of program. The chart on page 159 lists specific areas of IT covered in the activities; the accompanying text provides more detailed guidance on how to apply particular types of program.

Display ideas
In this section, ideas for display in the classroom are incorporated into the activity plans. It is important that displays often be interactive and 3-D.

Reference to photocopiable sheet(s)
Where activities include photocopiable sheets, small facsimiles of the relevant sheets are included in the lesson plans, with notes describing how they can be used.

Summative assessment
The design and make assignments (DMAs) allow teachers to make summative assessments of their children's design and technology capability. Using all the evidence which is collected throughout the DMA, such as observations of discussions, design drawings, modelling and the finished product, the teacher can assess the children against the level descriptions for designing and for making, deciding which level best fits or describes the work of each child.

Photocopiable sheets
Many of the activities are accompanied by photocopiable sheets. For some activities, there may be more than one version of the same sheet; or the sheet may be generic, with a facility for the teacher to choose the appropriate activity in order to provide differentiation by task. Other sheets may be more open and provide differentiation by outcome. The photocopiable sheets are useful for assessment purposes and can be kept as records in pupils' or level portfolios of work.

Cross-curricular links
Cross-curricular links are identified on a simple grid (on page 160) which cross-references particular areas of study in design and technology to the programmes of study for other subjects.

DESIGN AND TECHNOLOGY AT KEY STAGE 1

It is vital that young children be given experiences which will enable them to play a constructive part in our changing technological society. Design and technology provides a framework for such experiences. Before 1990, the subject existed in many forms and aspects were covered in a variety of curriculum areas; but from 1990, design and technology as an identified curriculum subject has been introduced into the curriculum in England and Wales through its inclusion in the National Curriculum. Its importance as a subject in the curriculum is manifold. It provides opportunities for children to learn through doing and talking; to be involved in problem solving; to acquire a flexible approach; to approach problems in real contexts; and to develop important personal qualities

and attitudes such as creativity, co-operation and perseverance.

The National Curriculum states that design and technology capability can be developed through 'combining designing and making skills with knowledge and understanding in order to design and make products'. The word 'combining' is important, as each aspect needs to be linked to a creative process through which the children will develop their capability. This process is neither linear nor cyclical, but has a number of elements to which the child will return throughout the whole process. The child should be developing the ability to identify a purpose for the product, develop his or her design proposal, modify it in the light of information gained from evaluation, plan how to implement the design proposal, make a high-quality product and evaluate the process that he or she has been through and the product that has been made. At various stages of the process, the communication of ideas is obviously important; a range of skills, including verbal, graphical and modelling skills, can be used to communicate the ideas. To make informed decisions about their own and others' products, the children need to be given opportunities to form value judgements relating to aesthetic, economic, moral, scientific, environmental and technical factors.

The knowledge and understanding that the children use support the development of a quality end product. Without appropriate knowledge of mechanisms, for example, the child will be unable to choose and incorporate an appropriate mechanism into his or her model. The knowledge may be developed in sessions identified as design and technology; but equally it may be developed in science, mathematics or

art, and the children can then draw on the knowledge when appropriate. This has implications for planning, and highlights the need for a whole-school approach in order for appropriate links across subject areas to be made. Just as design and technology draws on different areas of the curriculum, it also feeds into them.

To develop the children's capability, the National Curriculum Order sets out three types of activity in which they should be engaged. Investigate, disassemble and evaluate activities (IDEAs) should provide the children with opportunities to acquire knowledge and understanding (for example, of materials, structures and products). Focused practical tasks (FPTs) should provide activities in which the children can develop, for example, their making skills, using a range of tools and equipment. These two types of activity are inter-related and should provide opportunities for the children to develop the skills and knowledge which they need to carry out a design and make assignment (DMA).

At Key Stage 1, children need to be given opportunities to develop their capability through:
▲ the use of a range of materials including sheet material, reclaimed materials, textiles, food and construction kits;
▲ investigation of the working characteristics of materials;
▲ the application of skills, knowledge and understanding, particularly from science, maths, art and IT.

The development of designing skills is often neglected. These skills are vital if children are to produce a quality product which is fit for its purpose. The children need to develop and communicate their ideas through a range of methods and be able to evaluate these methods.

Making skills involve the development of the children's ability to select appropriate materials, tools and equipment; to assemble, join and combine these into a quality product; and to apply suitable finishing techniques. The children should be able to discuss the strengths and weaknesses of their products against their original criteria.

The knowledge base required at Key Stage 1 includes:
▲ structures;
▲ mechanisms;
▲ products and their application;
▲ quality;
▲ health and safety;
▲ vocabulary (through design and technology work, it is crucial that children be given opportunities to develop not only specific technical vocabulary, but also to develop a wider awareness of technological language).

Throughout their designing and making work, the children should be encouraged to think for themselves, to think critically, to make choices and decisions and to be creative. The activities should be relevant, realistic, purposeful and challenging, building on the children's previous skills and their knowledge and understanding. Design and technology should be fun and enjoyable – and certainly, there are many teachers and children who have already found this out for themselves.

Learning objective	PoS/AO	Content	Type of activity	Page
Structures				
To investigate what makes a structure more stable. To work co-operatively.	1c; 2c; 5b, c, g. **Technology** – Using the design process: Level B.	Building towers in different ways.	IDEA Small group.	14
To investigate what makes a wall stable. To work co-operatively.	1c; 2c; 5b, c, g. As above: Level B.	Building walls using different bonds.	IDEA Large or small group.	15
To investigate what makes a structure stable. To practise accurate cutting skills. To give a product a high-quality finish.	1b; 2c; 5b, g. As above: Level B.	Making an animal that will stand up.	FPT Large or small group.	16
To investigate stability. To investigate how to make something able to withstand greater loads.	1c; 2c; 5b, c, g. Effectiveness of design: Level B.	Investigating position and thickness of legs in relation to stability.	IDEA Large or small group.	18
To develop measuring and making skills. To practise evaluation and working co-operatively. To develop knowledge of rigidity in structures.	1b; 2a, b, c; 4a, b, c; 5b, f, g. As above: Level B.	Making a rigid frame for a picture.	FPT Small group.	19
To learn how to set up equipment. To develop the ability to use a saw safely. To develop modelling, designing and evaluation skills.	1b; 2a; 3; 4a, b, c; 5b, f, g. Practical skills, techniques and safe procedures: Level B.	Making a piece of furniture for a teddy or doll.	FPT Small group, in pairs.	21
To investigate ways of making paper and card stiffer by changing their shape.	1b; 2a, b, c; 4a, b, c; 5b,g. Properties of materials: Level B.	Decorating a mask using a range of folding and curling techniques.	FPT Large or small group.	23
Mechanisms				
To develop children's knowledge and understanding of mechanisms.	1c; 5a, c, d, g. Design and manufacture: Level B.	Investigating toys and how they move.	IDEA Class or large-group activity.	26
To develop children's knowledge and understanding of how wheels work.	1c; 5a, c, d, g. As above: Level B.	Investigating and disassembling toy vehicles to see how wheels work.	IDEA Small group.	27
To develop children's knowledge and understanding of a range of mechanisms and how they work.	1c; 2c; 5a, g. Selecting and using design processes: Level B.	Handing different mechanisms and making choices about appropriateness for purpose.	IDEA Class or large group.	28
To develop children's knowledge and understanding of the use of air to transmit force, and how air pressure can be harnessed to make things move.	1c; 2c; 5a, g. **Science** – Forces and their effects: Level B.	Investigating how syringes with tubing can be made to move up and down.	IDEA Class work, in small groups.	29
To develop knowledge and understanding of wheels and axles.	1b; 2a, c; 4; 5a, g. **Technology** – Practical skills and techniques: Level B.	Making vehicles with wheels that move.	FPT Small group, in pairs.	31
To develop the children's knowledge and understanding of how different mechanisms work. To develop the children's ability to make different mechanisms.	1b; 2a, c; 4; 5a, e, f, g. Selecting and using design processes: Level B.	Making and drawing different mechanisms.	FPT Small group.	32
To develop the children's understanding of how moving joints work. To develop the children's ability to join pieces of card.	1b; 2a, c; 3; 4; 5a, e, f, g. As above: Level B.	Making jointed puppets.	FPT Class or large group.	34
To develop the children's understanding of how pulley wheels and winding mechanisms can be used to help lift heavy loads. To develop the children's making skills.	1b; 2a, c; 4; 5a, c, f, g. As above: Level B.	Making a model that incorporates a pulley wheel to lift the cat out of the well.	FPT Small group.	35
To develop the children's understanding of pneumatic forces. To develop the children's making skills. To develop the children's ability to work co-operatively.	1b; 2a, c; 3; 4; 5a, e, f, g. As above: Level B.	Making a mouth that will open and close.	FPT Small group in pairs.	36
Reclaimed materials				
To develop the children's ability to sort materials against various criteria.	1c; 2b, c; 5g. **Science** – Materials from Earth: Level A.	Sorting a range of materials, using different criteria.	IDEA Large or small group.	38

9

DESIGN AND TECHNOLOGY

Learning objective	PoS/AO	Content	Type of activity	Page
To investigate the shapes of a range of reclaimed materials. To model ideas.	1c; 2c; 3a, b, c; 5g. As above: Level A.	Sorting a range of reclaimed materials and choosing appropriate shapes to make something of their choice.	IDEA Large or small group.	39
To investigate, disassemble and reassemble a box. To work together co-operatively.	1c; 2b; 5c, d, g. As above: Level A.	Turning boxes inside-out.	IDEA Large or small group.	40
To investigate and evaluate the features which make packaging attractive. To design an attractive exterior for a package.	1c; 3; 5c, d, g. As above: Level A.	Evaluating a range of packaging and creating an eye-catching one of their own.	IDEA Large or small group.	41
To know what a hinge is. To make a hinge in a variety of ways, using a variety of joiners. To develop co-operative working skills.	1b; 4; 5a, e, f, g. Practical skills and techniques: Level A.	Making different hinges.	FPT Class; large group; small group.	42
To investigate how well different structures withstand different loads.	1c; 2c; 5b, g. As above: Level A.	Testing boxes to find out if different faces withstand greater loads.	IDEA Class or large group.	44
To develop joining and finishing techniques.	1b; 2a, b; 3; 4; 5a, e, f, g. Using design processes: Level A.	Investigating different ways of joining thin surfaces and making something, using one/some of the techniques.	FPT Large or small group.	45
To develop knowledge and understanding of how well different glues and tapes join reclaimed materials. To use knowledge of how to use different-shaped materials for particular purposes. To work co-operatively.	1b; 2a, b, c; 3; 4; 5a, e, f, g. Properties of materials: Level A.	Investigating different glues and tapes and making a model, choosing appropriate joining materials.	FPT Large or small group.	46

Textiles

Learning objective	PoS/AO	Content	Type of activity	Page
To develop children's familiarity with different fastenings and their uses.	1c; 2c; 5c, g. Effectiveness of design: Level A.	Physically exploring different fastenings and deciding on their uses.	IDEA Whole class working in groups.	50
To develop children's understanding that the shape, size and material of a bag depends on its purpose.	1c; 2b; 5c, d, g. As above: Level A.	Examining and evaluating a collection of bags.	IDEA Class but individual recording.	51
To develop children's knowledge and understanding of how different fabrics are made in different ways, have different properties and are suitable for different purposes.	1c; 2b, c; 5g. Properties of materials: Level A.	Observing and sorting a range of fabrics.	IDEA Class or group.	53
To develop the children's skill in evaluating a ready-made product.	1c; 5c, d, g. Effectiveness of design: Level A.	Evaluating a collection of hats.	IDEA Large group work.	54
To develop the children's practical skill in making different joins with fabrics.	1b; 2a; 4; 5e, f, g. Practical skills and techniques: Level A.	Joining fabrics in different ways and displaying their examples.	FPT Large or small group.	55
To develop the children's knowledge and understanding of a pattern and how to use it. To develop and extend their ability to cut out accurately.	1b; 2a; 4; 5e, f, g. As above: Level A.	Looking at and using a pattern to cut out a piece of clothing for a collage.	FPT Class discussion groups.	56
To develop and extend the children's knowledge and understanding of patterns. To develop their ability to join fabrics and produce a quality finish.	1b; 2a; 4; 5e, f, g. As above: Level A.	Making a comb or pencil case, using a pattern and joining fabric.	FPT Small group.	58
To develop the children's awareness of how decoration (such as printing and painting) can enhance the look of fabric. To develop the children's ability to decorate fabric.	1b; 2a; 3; 4d; 5e, f, g. As above: Level A.	Making a picture on fabric using different techniques such as printing.	FPT Class discussion groups.	59
To develop children's knowledge and understanding of how fabrics can be made by weaving. To develop their ability to weave.	1b; 2a, b; 3; 4; 5c, e, g. Design and manufacture: Level A.	Disassembling a piece of woven material and weaving one.	FPT Small group work.	60
To develop the children's knowledge and understanding of different stitches and their uses.	1b; 2a; 5e, f, g. Selecting and using design processes: Level A.	Making a bookmark using different stitches.	FPT Small group.	61

DESIGN AND TECHNOLOGY

Overview grid

Learning objective	PoS/AO	Content	Type of activity	Page
Food				
To develop knowledge and understanding of safe and hygienic working.	1c; 5f. *Safe procedures: Level A.*	Safe and hygienic ways of working with food.	IDEA Class or group.	64
To develop awareness that foods have different tastes and textures. To develop appropriate vocabulary to describe different textures and tastes.	1c; 2c; 3a, b; 5f, g. *Science: Living things and the processes of life: Level A.*	Testing different foods to explore tastes and textures.	IDEA Small group.	65
To develop awareness of the structure of a sandwich.	1c; 2b; 3a, b; 5c, d, f, g. *As above: Level A.*	Disassembling sandwiches.	IDEA Whole class.	67
To develop understanding that people have different preferences with regard to sandwich fillings. To introduce children to the idea of a survey and its function.	1c; 5c, d, g. *As above: Level A.*	Organising a survey to find out people's preferences.	IDEA Whole class.	68
To develop practical skills including the ability to combine and weigh ingredients. To develop an understanding of the need to follow instructions from a recipe.	1b; 2a, b, c; 3; 4; 5e, f, g. *As above: Level A.*	Making buns.	FPT Small group.	70
To understand the importance of the visual presentation of food.	1b; 2a, b; 3; 4; 5e, g. *As above: Level A.*	Using different colours, shapes and textures.	FPT Class or group.	71
Construction kits				
To investigate the movement of wheels and their attachment to a chassis. To create something that moves on wheels. To develop the children's ability to disassemble and reassemble.	1c; 2a, 5c, g. *Technology: The Design Process – Selecting and using design processes: Level B.*	Disassembling and reassembling model vehicles.	IDEA Large or small group.	74
To develop the children's ability to make judgements about a product. To develop their ability to work co-operatively.	1c; 2a; 5c, d, g. *Effectiveness of design in systems...: Level B.*	Looking critically at a kit.	IDEA Small group.	75
To develop understanding of stability. To develop the practical ability to join materials in different ways. To develop the children's ability to evaluate their own products.	1b; 2a; 3; 4; 5b, e. g. *Selecting and using design processes: Level B.*	Making climbing frames.	FPT Small group in pairs.	77
To develop understanding of rigid shapes and their importance in supporting structures.	1b; 2a, c; 5g. *As above: Level B.*	Making different shapes including triangles.	FPT Large or small group.	78
To develop children's understanding of a construction kit through investigation. To develop the children's ability to form mental images.	1c; 2a, c; 3; 4; 5c, d, g. *Properties of materials and tools...: Level A.*	Selecting different pieces to make a variety of models.	IDEA Small group.	79
To develop children's investigative skills. To extend their understanding of mechanisms.	1c; 2a; 5a, c, g. *Effectiveness of design in systems...: Level B.*	Looking at different mechanisms to see how they work.	IDEA Small group.	80
To develop the children's ability to follow instructions.	1b; 2a; 5a, g. *Design and manufacturing processes: Level B.*	Working through a sequence to make a model.	FPT Large or small group.	81
Electricity				
To investigate what components are needed to make a circuit. To explore, through disassembly, how components are put together to make a circuit. To work together co-operatively. To talk to an audience and listen to others.	1c; 5c, g. *Science: Energy and Forces – Properties and uses of energy: Level C.*	Disassembling a torch.	IDEA Large or small group.	84
To construct an electrical circuit. To work together co-operatively.	1c; 2a; 4c; 5g. *As above: Level C.*	Making a circuit.	FPT Large or small group.	85
To be able to put a switch in a circuit. To be aware of the purpose of the switch and its ability to make or break the circuit.	1c; 2a; 4c; 5g. *As above: Level C.*	Putting a switch into a circuit.	IDEA Large or small group.	87
To be able to make an electrical switch. To develop co-operative working skills. To develop the ability to follow instructions.	1b; 2a; 4c; 5e, g. *As above: Level C.*	Making a switch.	FPT Large or small group.	88

DESIGN AND TECHNOLOGY

Learning objective	PoS/AO	Content	Type of activity	Page
To develop skills of evaluation and comparison. To develop awareness that different people have different needs and preferences.	1c; 5c, g. *As above: Level C.*	Evaluating toys.	IDEA Class or large group.	89
To be aware of the dangers of playing with electricity. To make something with a mechanism. To work together co-operatively.	1b; 2a; 4; 5a, e, f, g. *As above: Level C.*	Making a safety poster with moving parts.	FPT Small group.	90
To develop children's skill in making circuits with switches. To extend their ability to follow instructions and work co-operatively.	1b. *As above: Level C.*	Putting a circuit and a switch into a model.	FPT Small group, in pairs.	91
Mouldable materials				
To develop the children's investigative skills.	1c; 2a, b, c; 5g. *Science: Earth and Space – Materials from Earth: Level C.*	Investigating clay and its properties.	IDEA Class or large group.	94
To develop the children's evaluative skills.	1c; 2a; 5c, d, g. *As above: Level C.*	Evaluating a collection of objects.	IDEA Class or large group.	95
To develop the children's skills of disassembly and investigation.	1c; 2a, b, c; 5c, g. *As above: Level C.*	Investigating papier mâché.	IDEA Large or small group.	96
To develop the children's investigative and disassembly skills.	1c; 2a, b, c; 4; 5f, g. *As above: Level C.*	Making dough.	IDEA Large or small group.	98
To develop the children's skills of making, including shaping and finishing.	1b. *As above: Level C.*	Moulding, shaping and finishing dough models.	FPT Large group.	99
To develop the children's making skills, particularly in shaping and finishing. To develop their design skills, particularly relating to pattern and the use of colour.	1b; 2a, b, c; 3c; 4; 5e, f, g. *As above: Level C.*	Making clay pots.	FPT Large group.	100
To develop children's understanding that wire can be bent into many shapes, then returned almost to its original shape.	1b; 2a, b; 3a, b, c; 4; 5e, g. *As above: Level C.*	Modelling with pipe cleaners.	FPT Class or large group.	102
To develop the children's designing, making and evaluative skills.	1b; 2a, b, c; 3; 4; 5e, g. *As above: Level C.*	Making a papier mâché pot and finishing it.	FPT Group.	103
Design and make assignments				
To design and make a shelter for a purpose. To make a stable structure.	1a; 2a, b, c; 3; 4; 5a, d, e, f, g. *Technology: The Design Process – Selecting and using design processes: Level B.*	Making a shelter.	Individual.	107
To design and make a village bus which will not get stuck on a muddy road. To demonstrate the ability to select appropriate wheels for a model vehicle. To demonstrate the ability to attach wheels so that they can turn.	1a; 2a, b, c; 3; 4; 5b, d, e, f, g. *Effectiveness of design: Level B.*	Making a bus that will not get stuck in the mud.	Individual.	108
To design and make a bag for a particular purpose. To choose appropriate finishing techniques for the bag.	1a; 2a, b, c; 3; 4; 5b, d, e, f, g. *Selecting and using design processes: Level B.*	Making a bag for a purpose.	Individual.	109
To design and make sweets for a particular purpose. To choose appropriate shapes, colours and flavours for the sweets.	1a; 2a, b, c; 3; 4; 5d, e, f, g. *As above: Level B.*	Making sweets for a purpose.	Individual.	110
To design and make a chart for representing weather. To choose appropriate mechanisms for moving parts on the chart.	1a; 2a, b, c; 3; 4; 5a, d, e, f, g. *As above: Level B.*	Making a weather chart.	Individual.	112
To design and make a jointed puppet. To choose how to finish the puppet.	1a; 2a, b, c; 3; 4; 5a, d, e, f, g. *Design and manufacturing: Level A.*	Making a puppet.	Individual.	113
To design and make a gift from clay for a particular person.	1a; 2a, b, c; 3; 4; 5d, e, f, g. *As above: Level A.*	Making a gift.	Individual.	114
To design and make a room.	1a; 2a, b, c; 3; 4; 5b, d, e, f, g. *As above: Level A.*	Making a room.	Pairs.	115

Entries given in italics relate to the Scottish 5–14 Guidelines for Technology.

DESIGN AND TECHNOLOGY

Structures

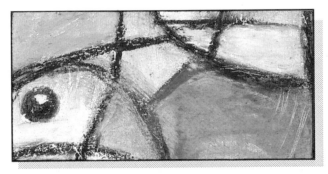

This chapter of the book contains investigate, disassemble and evaluate activities (IDEAs) and focused practical tasks (FPTs) relating to structures.

Through this work, children will have the opportunity to design and make products which incorporate structures and to acquire knowledge and understanding relating the principles of stability and strength to appropriate technical vocabulary and issues of safety.

The designing skills developed in this chapter include discussion of ideas, modelling of ideas using wood strips and card, drawing of designs and evaluation of design ideas. Making skills developed here include cutting, sawing, joining, finishing and evaluation of finished products. The knowledge and understanding developed concerns the investigation of stability, the strengthening of a material by changing its shape, the making of a structure to withstand greater loads, the evaluation of structures for a purpose, the need for safe handling of tools and safe working methods, and the importance of using correct vocabulary.

The children can start by exploring their own school environment for a range of structures, before exploring structures in the local environment and in an environment which contrasts with their own. Appropriate contexts for work with structures include: houses and homes, animals, packaging, shops and shopping, containers and the playground.

⚠ It is essential that when the children are cutting and joining materials, they handle and use the tools correctly.

Links should be made between these activities and tasks relating to structures in the chapters on Reclaimed materials, Textiles and Construction kits.

DESIGN AND
TECHNOLOGY

TOWER OF STRENGTH `IDEA`

To investigate what makes a structure more stable. To work co-operatively.

†† *Small groups (depending on the amount of equipment available).*

🕐 *30 minutes.*

Previous skills/knowledge needed
Links can be made with the activity 'Let's stick together'.

Key background information
The lower the centre of mass is in an object, the more stable a structure is. If there is more mass at the top, then it is easier to push something over. It is important for the children to have a variety of activities, using different contexts in which they investigate structures with wide bases, to help them understand this concept.

Language to be introduced
base, wide, structure, build

Preparation
Make sure that there are sufficient construction kit bricks for the children to work with.

Resources needed
Building blocks, a collection of balls, a piece of wood for a ramp, one copy per child of photocopiable sheet 118.

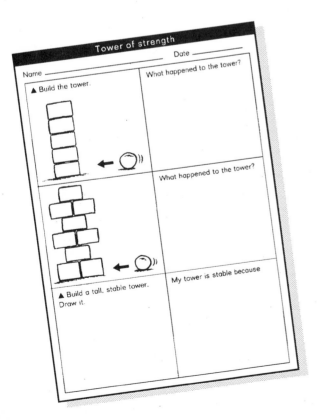

What to do
Ask the children to work in pairs within their groups to build the tallest tower they can by placing the bricks one on top of another. The height they reach will depend on how many bricks, and what type of bricks, they have. It is likely that they will not be able to build as tall a tower with smooth bricks as with bricks that fasten together (such as LEGO).

When the tower is finished, ask the children how they can find out whether it is stable or can easily be knocked or blown down. Discuss their ideas and set up an investigation. The children might suggest rolling a ball at the base, rolling a ball down a ramp or blowing at the tower. They may need to think about trying each method more than once. Give them copies of photocopiable sheet 118 on which to record the result.

Now ask them to build a tower with a wider base, such as the one shown on photocopiable sheet 118, and try their investigation again. Ask them to record their results on their sheet by drawing and/or writing. Discuss with the children which tower was harder to make fall over. Talk about the wide base and how it helped to make the tower more stable. Ask them to build a tall, stable tower and draw it on the last part of the photocopiable sheet.

Suggestion(s) for extension
The children can think about how to make their test fair: the same method of testing, the same distance, the same number of bricks?

The children can write up their investigation with conclusions based on the evidence.

DESIGN AND TECHNOLOGY

The bottom part of the sheet is left for them to draw their own design for a tall, stable tower (after building it). They can write down why they think this tower will be stable.

LET'S STICK TOGETHER IDEA

To investigate what helps to make a wall stable.
To work co-operatively.

†† *Large or small group, working in pairs.*

🕐 *30 minutes.*

Previous skills/knowledge needed
This activity links with the activity 'Tower of strength' (page 14).

Key background information
Overlapping bricks (or any such items) creates a more stable structure than placing one on top of another. The bricks are bonded together by overlapping. Bonding provides a uniting force; it does not mean that the bricks are stuck together, though in a real brick wall cement is used to provide extra cohesion.

Language to be introduced
bond, overlap, wall, brick, stable, unstable

Preparation
Collect together enough building bricks (duplo, LEGO or similar) for a group of children working in pairs to make two small walls.

Suggestion(s) for support
A peer or adult may need to build two towers, one with a wider base, and discuss with individual children why a wider base makes something more stable.

Assessment opportunities
The comments that the children make will show whether they have an understanding of stability. Their recording will show whether they are able to record results systematically.

Opportunities for IT
The children can draw their own shape towers using a simple drawing package, or framework software such as 'My World 2' with a suitable shapes file. They could then print the pictures, and build the models to find which is the most stable. Such activities will also give young children opportunities to use the mouse and develop hand-eye co-ordination.

Display ideas
The children can draw round the bricks, cut them out and paste them onto a large sheet of paper to show which was the most stable tower that they built, and to show a less stable tower collapsing.

Reference to photocopiable sheet
When they have built the tower with a narrow base, the children can fill in the top part of the sheet to show how they tried to make it fall over. When they have tried to make the tower with the wider base fall down, they can record the result of the investigation in the middle part of the sheet.

DESIGN AND TECHNOLOGY

Resources needed

Bricks, a collection of balls, one copy per child of photocopiable sheet 119.

What to do

Give the children copies of photocopiable sheet 119. Ask them to work in pairs, building the two walls shown in the pictures. While they are making these walls, talk with them about the arrangement of the bricks and use the words 'brick', 'bond' and 'overlap'. When they have completed the walls, ask them to push each wall gently. Discuss with them which one they think is more stable (less easily moved) and why this is.

Then make sure that the group can see you roll a ball against each wall in turn. The wall that is in separate columns should move or fall over more easily than the brick bonded wall. Again, ask the children for ideas about why one wall seems more stable than the other. They may comment that the overlapping helps the bricks to stick together. Now ask them to fill in the second part of photocopiable sheet 119.

Suggestion(s) for extension

Take the children somewhere in the school grounds where they can see a brick wall. Compare it with the walls that they have built. Ask them to draw the wall.

The children could try different bonding patterns, using bricks end-on as well as sideways, and devise an investigation to find out which pattern is the most stable.

Suggestion(s) for support

Some children may need help with fitting the bricks together in the right pattern. Further discussion may be needed to help them understand the difference in the ways the bricks are put together and the difference this makes to the stability of the wall.

Assessment opportunities

From the comments that the children make and their drawing and writing on photocopiable sheet 119, it will be possible to assess whether the children understand what helps to make a wall stable.

Opportunities for IT

The children could use a simple drawing package or framework software such as 'My World 2' to draw the pattern of their bonded walls. If they are given a choice of two types of block, they can drag these blocks to make suitably bonded walls so that the joints do not overlap.

Display ideas

Make some brick rubbings and display these to show the arrangement of bricks in a wall. Make labels with the words 'overlap' and 'brick bond' to reinforce the meaning of the words.

Display the two types of wall that the children have made, together with some of their completed photocopiable sheets.

Reference to photocopiable sheet

Give out the sheet at the beginning of the activity, so that the children can use the pictures of walls to follow in building their own. The children will draw the more stable wall on the bottom part of the sheet.

STANDING STILL ◆ FPT

To investigate what makes a structure stable. To practise accurate cutting skills. To give a product a high-quality finish.

†† *Large or small group.*

⏱ *Session 1: 30 minutes. Session 2: 20–30 minutes. These sessions can be carried out at different times.*

Previous skills/knowledge needed

It will be helpful if the children can cut out with scissors, but the activity gives practice in this skill.

Key background information

This activity is different from 'Tower of strength' and 'Let's stick together' in that it gives the children a specific experience of making something that is stable, not just of investigating what makes something stable.

Standing still

▲ Cut out the shapes.
▲ Cut along the dotted lines.

Language to be introduced

stable, stability, stand up, slot

Preparation

Make copies of photocopiable sheet 120 onto thin card. Cut out the pictures from one copy, ready to show the children. Decide how the children will finish the animal (colour it, cover it with tissue paper or fabric, and so on) and collect the materials that are needed. Find a soft toy with four legs that will stand up.

Resources needed

A soft toy (see above); masking tape; one card copy per child of photocopiable sheet 120, and one cut-out animal (see above); one pair of scissors per child; finishing items such as glue, coloured crayons and pens, scraps of fabric, tissue paper.

What to do

Session 1

Put the soft toy on a table, so that all the children can see it. Ask the children why they think the toy can stand up, and push it gently to show how stable it is. They may suggest that it has four legs, that the legs are wide apart or that the legs are fat. Collect the children's ideas and ask questions to clarify them.

Then show the children what happens when the toy does not have four legs to stand on. Try folding up opposite legs under the animal, then legs on the same side of the body, and fix them in place each time with masking tape. Before the animal is placed on the table, ask the children to predict what will happen. Gently push the animal and show the children that it is not so stable or that it cannot stand up. Ask the children to come to some conclusions about stability. They may suggest that the legs need to be at the same place on each side; that the animal has to have two on one side to balance the two on the other; or that the animal has to have legs that are as wide as the body. Tell the children that they are going to make a card (imaginary) animal that can stand up. Then show the children the cut-out body from

DESIGN AND TECHNOLOGY

photocopiable sheet 120 and ask them how they could make it stand up. Try out their suggestions if possible (or suggest that they try them out at another time). Show them how the legs slot onto the body, and how the animal will now stand up. Hand out photocopiable sheet 120 and talk with the children about what they will do. If they are not going to give the animal figure a finish immediately, tell them where to keep the animal meanwhile (for instance, in a folder or tray). End the session by looking at the animal and asking the children again why they think it stands up.

Session 2

The children are going to finish their animals by decorating them. Discuss with them what they may want to put on the outline (such as eyes, nose, ears, hooves). Tell or remind them how important it is to give the item a high-quality finish, whatever they use. Tell them to clear away when they have finished their animals.

Suggestion(s) for extension

Ask the children to make something else out of card that will stand up on its own. This could be linked to a topic, a character from a book or different animals.

Suggestion(s) for support

Individual children may need further experience working with the soft toy to understand why it is stable. They can try the soft toy activity for themselves.

Help may be needed with cutting out and slotting the card animal together.

Assessment opportunities

From the children's comments, it will be possible to assess their understanding of what makes something stable. The finished card animal will show whether they can cut out neatly and add a quality finish.

Opportunities for IT

The children could use a simple drawing or art package to create a shape which can be printed, cut out and made to stand up. The children could experiment with a symmetrical shape which could be copied and then flipped to make a matching shape. This can be printed and then folded in two down the line of symmetry.

Display ideas

The children can create a suitable tabletop environment in which to display the finished animals.

Reference to photocopiable sheet

After the discussion, the children will cut out the body and the two leg pieces and then cut in the slots. Remind the children not to cut all the way and end up with seven pieces of card!

IS THE TABLE STABLE?

To investigate stability. To investigate how to make something able to withstand greater loads.

†† *Large or small group, working in pairs.*

🕐 *30 minutes.*

Previous skills/knowledge needed

This activity has links with 'Standing still' (page 16).

Key background information

By using a mouldable material, the children can change a shape quickly to make something more stable and able to withstand greater loads. Plasticine is more suitable than play dough for this activity, because it is stiffer and more able to support loads.

Language to be introduced

balance, stable, stability, roll, mould, Plasticine

Preparation

Ensure that the Plasticine will mould easily, and that there is enough for the group to work with. Collect some boards or pieces of stiff plastic sheet for the children to work on.

Resources needed

Plasticine, boards or pieces of stiff plastic sheet, one copy per child of photocopiable sheet 121.

DESIGN AND TECHNOLOGY

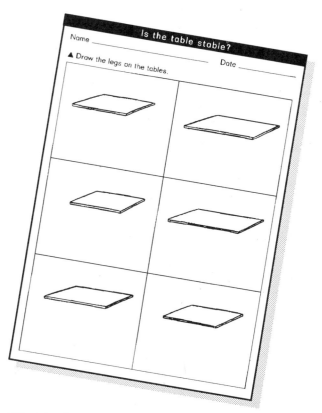

Name _____
Is the table stable?
▲ Draw the legs on the tables.
Date _____

What to do

Ask the children, working in pairs, to flatten out a piece of Plasticine so that it is a square with sides about 6–8cm. Make one yourself. Ask the children to investigate different ways of supporting the square so that it will stand up like a table. Ask them to think about the following questions:

▲ How many legs are needed?
▲ Where do the legs need to be?
▲ How thick should the legs be?
▲ Is there only one way of making the table stand up?

Ask the children to record each solution on photocopiable sheet 121 by drawing and labelling their model. Allow time for investigation before you have a discussion with the children about what they have found out. Some of their ideas may be:

▲ the legs need to be near the edge;
▲ thin legs do not support as well as thick legs;
▲ four legs make something more stable than two legs.

Suggestion(s) for extension

The children could draw designs for their models and predict which models will be stable and which will not, before making them to test their predictions.

Make up a book of pictures of furniture, perhaps from catalogues. Ask the children to annotate it with their ideas about why the furniture is stable.

Suggestion(s) for support

An adult may need to make just two or three models to show the children, and make the differences very clear to some individual children.

Assessment opportunities

From the discussion and recording, it will be possible to assess the children's ideas relating to strength and stability.

Opportunities for IT

The children could use a word processor to write an explanation of their plan for a stable table. They could use a large font, so that the explanation can be displayed alongside the Plasticine table they have made.

Display ideas

Display the models with some of the completed photocopiable sheets. Add labels with questions such as *Which table do you think is most stable? Which table would hold the most mass?*

Reference to photocopiable sheet

The children will need to have copies of page 121 at the beginning of the activity. They could all fill in the first box together to make sure that they understand how to use the sheet. Remind them to keep the Plasticine away from the photocopiable sheet, to keep the paper clean.

IN THE FRAME   FPT

To develop measuring and making skills. To practise evaluation and working co-operatively. To develop knowledge of rigidity in structures.

†† *Small group.*
🕓 *Session 1: 45–60 minutes. Session 2: 20–30 minutes.*
⚠ *Make sure that the children know how to use the equipment and are closely supervised when they are sawing.*

Previous skills/knowledge needed

The children will need to be able to saw wood, as in the activity 'Sawing wood' (page 21). They should also have previous knowledge of what makes something rigid, as in the activity 'A rigid shape' (page 78); and of how to join materials, as in the activity 'Anyone can join' (page 34).

Key background information

When the children have made the frame, it will be rigid, the sides being held in place by the card triangles.

Language to be introduced

frame, junior hacksaw, G-clamp, bench hook, sandpaper, triangle

Preparation

Make sure that there is one G-clamp, one bench hook and one saw between two children. Cut up sandpaper into 4cm

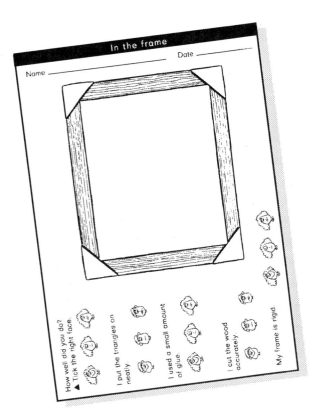

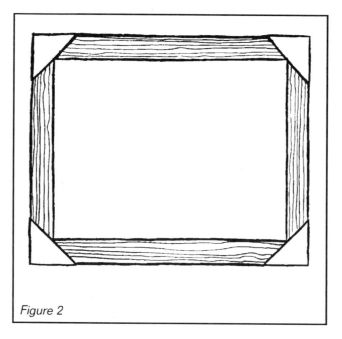

Figure 2

can remember about how to cut wood and how to finish the ends properly. One or two children can give a demonstration. Show the children how they will measure 12cm with a ruler and mark it with a pencil before they cut each piece. Check that the children understand what will go wrong if they cut different-sized pieces of wood for opposite sides of the frame. Then show the children how they will join the pieces together with card triangles to make a frame (see Figure 2). Remind them that they only need a small amount of glue: the more glue, the less stick.

squares and check that there is sufficient wood for each child to have a 50cm strip of wood. Make a set of card triangles (see Figure 1). Make sure that there are enough copies to provide for eight triangles per child (or get out card triangles from your store). Find a picture frame, preferably a wooden one.

Resources needed

Card triangles (see Figure 1), scissors, glue and spreaders, G-clamps, junior hacksaws, bench hooks, sandpaper, one copy per child of photocopiable sheet 122.

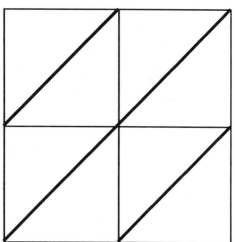

Figure 1

What to do

Session 1

Show the children the picture frame, and discuss with them how it is rigid and cannot change shape. Explain that they are going to make a frame with wood strips. Ask what they

DESIGN AND TECHNOLOGY

As the children are working, encourage them to saw and sandpaper alternately so that they can take turns with the saw. When the frames are finished, the children should leave them to dry. Ask them to write their names on the frames. Either now or at a later time, they can create pictures to go in their frames.

Session 2
When the frames are dry, give them back to the children at their tables. Ask them to push the frames gently, all ways, to find out if they are rigid. What do they think helps to make them rigid?

Then look at the quality of the finish. Ask the children to check that they have cut all the lengths of wood the same size, that they have used a small amount of glue, that the triangles were put neatly onto all four corners and that there are no dirty fingermarks on the frame. The children can then fill in the evaluation sheet (page 122).

Suggestion(s) for extension
The children can choose their own lengths, then add a stand to the frame to make it stand upright on its own.

Suggestion(s) for support
Some children may need support through additional questioning to understand why the frame is rigid. Some may need help with sawing and with placing the triangles at the corners. Encourage the children to support each other before seeking adult help.

Assessment opportunities
From the children's comments, it will be possible to assess their ideas about what makes the frame rigid. From the finished products, it will be possible to assess their ability to measure accurately, to saw and to join neatly.

Opportunities for IT
The children could use an art package to draw their own picture to fit inside the frame they have made. Alternatively, they could use a word processor to write a set of instructions for making the frame which could be used by another child. This would enable them to focus on the sequence of events, and to redraft their work to make sure the instructions are in the right order. Children may need to be shown how to use the 'cut and paste' or 'drag and drop' commands to move parts of their text around the correct sequence.

Display ideas
Mount samples of the materials used to make the frames on a background, and display the finished frames (with pictures inserted) around this.

Reference to photocopiable sheet
At the end of the activity, the children should use photocopiable sheet 122 to give their final evaluation of their frame. Encourage them to be honest and accurate.

SAWING WOOD `FPT`

To learn how to set up equipment. To develop the ability to use a saw safely. To develop modelling, designing and evaluation skills.

†† *Small group, working in pairs.*

🕐 *45 minutes.*

⚠ *Make sure that the children know how to use the equipment, and are not left unsupervised when they are sawing.*

Key background information
It is essential, when children are introduced to sawing wood, that they learn the correct way of setting up and using the equipment. They will need to be taught how to clamp the bench hook onto the table and how to hold the saw. It may be necessary for the teacher to clamp the bench hook in place, but the children can still be shown how to do it.

There are a range of possible alternatives to the bench hook, such as a sawing jig or a Richardson block (see Figure 3). There are advantages to each of these; use whichever is available or you feel is best for the children. Make sure that the children carry out a gentle backwards and forwards movement to saw the wood. Children will often 'cut into' wood as though it were Plasticine. Always sandpaper the sawn end of the piece of wood after sawing, to smooth any

Structures

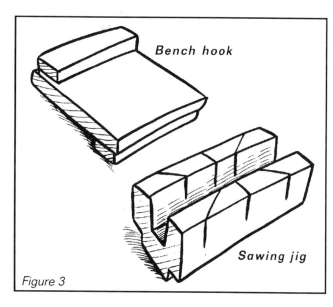

Bench hook

Sawing jig

Figure 3

rough edges. To prevent the children rubbing away too much, show them how to rub each side once, gently, before going onto the next side.

Language to be introduced

bench hook, junior hacksaw, wood, sandpaper, G-clamp, glue, furniture, frame, shell

Preparation

Make sure that there is enough equipment to provide one clamp, one bench hook and one saw between two children. Check that the blades in the saws are not blunt, and cut the sandpaper into squares of side about 4cm. Put out one strip of wood (approx 50cm) for each pair. Decide on the length

for the pieces of wood to be used as measures – about 6cm to 8cm, depending on the size of the teddy or doll to be used – and cut one piece of wood to that length for each group.

Resources needed

10mm square, 50cm long strips of soft wood (one per pair), G-clamps, junior hacksaws, sandpaper, PVA glue or clear wood glue, glue spreaders, Blu-Tack or masking tape, a small teddy or doll, card, scissors, pieces of wood to be used as measures, scrap card, good quality card, one copy per child of photocopiable sheet 123.

What to do

Show the children the equipment and explain that they are going to learn how to saw wood. Each pair will have one strip of wood, and they can saw it up and make a piece of furniture with it for the teddy or doll. Show the children how to fix the clamp to the table, how to put the wood in the bench hook, how to saw and finally how to sandpaper the edges. Let one or two pupils try, so the others can see how it is done. The children need to saw four pieces of wood that are the same length, and then use these to make a piece of furniture (stool, chair, table, bed and so on). The wood strips will be the frame, and they can add card to make the shell. It is important that the children understand that the pieces need to be the same size – otherwise the furniture will not be stable. Ask them to look at their tables and chairs and see that the legs on each are of equal size.

The children can saw the wood alternately, so that each child saws two pieces. As one is sawing, the other can sandpaper the edges. When they have sawn the pieces, they can begin to model with the wood, fixing on scraps of

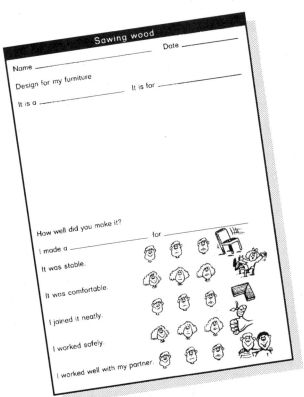

DESIGN AND
TECHNOLOGY

card with Blu-Tack or masking tape so they can see what the finished product might look like. Remind them that the teddy or doll needs to be able to use the piece of furniture comfortably. They may want to saw some other lengths with the wood that they have left over to complete their furniture. When they are satisfied with their modelling, ask them each to draw their design on photocopiable sheet 123. Then they can construct the actual piece of furniture and glue the pieces together. Remind the children to use a small amount of glue. When the piece of furniture is finished, ask them to evaluate their work, using the final section of photocopiable sheet 123.

Suggestion(s) for extension

The children can measure out their own pieces of wood and construct objects other than furniture.

Suggestion(s) for support

The children may need help with sawing to make sure that they understand the technique required.

Some children may need help to answer the questions on the evaluation sheet.

Assessment opportunities

From watching the children, it will be evident who can handle the equipment and who can saw properly. From the children's responses, evidence can be gathered of which children have an understanding of stability. From the final product, children's skills of cutting and shaping can be assessed.

Opportunities for IT

The children could use a word processor to write a list of

instructions on how to saw wood safely. They could experiment with different fonts and sizes, so that the final list can be displayed in the classroom as a reminder to others.

Display ideas

Make a collage of furniture, using pictures from catalogues.

Display the toy furniture, with the teddy bears or dolls using it, in front of the collage.

If it is practical, display the clamp, bench hook and saw and put up labels to remind the children how they are used.

Reference to photocopiable sheet

The children will need to be given photocopiable sheet 123 when they have finished modelling their design. They can then draw what they have modelled before making it. At the end of the activity, they will need guidance on how to record the evaluation of their product. They can be encouraged to add the teddy bears' or dolls' comments on the furniture, perhaps written around the display.

CHANGING THE SHAPE

To investigate ways of making paper and card stiffer by changing their shape.

†† *Large or small group.*

🕐 *45–60 minutes.*

Key background information

The children will work with card and a variety of papers including tissue, crêpe and sugar paper. They will need to be given the opportunity to try different techniques in order to see and feel the changes in the materials.

Language to be introduced

tissue paper, crêpe paper, sugar paper, curl, tuft, crumple, fold, bend

Preparation

Draw a mask shape on an A4 sheet and photocopy it. Crumple, tuft, fold, bend and curl different papers and cards as examples to show the children. Collect a range of papers and cards in various colours.

Resources needed

Scrap and 'best' pieces of card; sugar, crêpe and tissue paper; Pritt sticks, scissors, PVA glue and spreaders; mask outlines (see above).

What to do

Discuss with the children how a flat piece of paper looks and feels. Then crumple some tissue paper and ask the children to press on it lightly. They should feel that it could now support some weight and is stiffer than before. Continue with each technique: folding, tufting and curling. Talk about the changes that can be seen and felt, and how the paper is strengthened and can stand up as a result of being bent and folded.

Now allow the children time to experiment with scraps of paper and card and to feel the changes made to them. Explain that they are going to use the different techniques to cover a mask, and ask the children for their ideas about which technique would be appropriate for each part of the mask. Give out the mask shapes and make sure that the children understand what they have to do. Check that they are cutting out and making the parts carefully and sticking with a small amount of glue, using differently-shaped pieces of paper and card to give a raised finish. They should leave the finished masks to dry.

Bring the session to a conclusion by showing some of the masks and discussing how appropriate some of the techniques are for specific parts of the mask. Examples might include crumpling for big cheeks, curling or folding for hair and tufting for the nose. Holes can be punched and string put through later.

Suggestion(s) for extension

The children can use these techniques to finish other models.

Suggestion(s) for support

The children could be introduced to one technique for shaping paper at a time.

Assessment opportunities

The children's comments about the changes to the paper and card can be noted. Watch and assess the children's skills when they are cutting and joining the paper and card. Look at the end product to see if they can produce a quality finish.

Opportunities for IT

The children could use an art package to draw their own design for a mask. They could go on to apply colours in order to make the mask more interesting. If they use a drawing program for this work, they could also add their own instructions on making different effects for different parts of the mask (for example, 'use crumpled tissue paper for this effect').

Display ideas

Make a display of the finished masks. Put large examples of each of the paper-shaping techniques around the edge of the display and label them.

DESIGN AND TECHNOLOGY

Mechanisms

Through working on the activities in this chapter, children will have opportunities to design and make products which incorporate mechanisms and to acquire knowledge and understanding relating to a range of mechanisms, safety issues and appropriate vocabulary.

The lesson plans aim to develop and extend children's designing skills including discussion of ideas, modelling of ideas (using a range of materials), drawing of designs and evaluation of ideas. The development of their making skills focuses on measuring, cutting, joining, finishing, evaluating their own and others' products and using appropriate tools and equipment.

The knowledge and understanding covered here includes investigating different mechanisms and how they work; disassembling mechanisms to find out how the parts fit together; evaluating mechanisms to decide which is fit for a particular purpose; and developing an understanding that a range of mechanisms have been used in the past, and that safety and the correct use of technical vocabulary are important.

Apart from wheels and joints, which are referred to in the Programme of Study, it is left for the teacher to decide which mechanisms (if any) the children should experience and work with. Understanding the concept that a mechanism helps us to move things and to do work is more important than experiencing specific mechanisms.

The following contexts are appropriate for work with mechanisms: toys, puppets, celebrations, transport, the playground, the fairground, moving about and stories.

⚠ When the children are cutting and joining materials, they must handle and use the tools correctly.

DESIGN AND
TECHNOLOGY

MAKE A MOVE   ◆ FPT

To develop children's knowledge and understanding of mechanisms.

†† *Class or large group.*

🕐 *30–45 minutes.*

Previous skills/knowledge needed

It is important to link this activity with others which focus on mechanisms, thus allowing the children to make comparisons between different kinds of movement.

Key background information

A mechanism is used to help us move things and do work. A mechanism is made up of parts that fit together to allow movement.

Language to be introduced

mechanism, movement

The specific language needed will vary depending on the mechanisms in the toy collection.

Preparation

Make a chart on which to record the mechanisms in the toys. (See Figure 1.) Make a collection of toys with different mechanisms, such as a wheel and axle, joint, spring, lever, slide, pneumatic device. Some of the toys could be made from construction kits in school.

Figure 1

Resources needed

A collection of toys (six to eight) which have a range of mechanisms; a chart (see above).

What to do

Seat the children in a circle, either on the floor or around a table, and put out the collection of toys. Tell the children that they are going to investigate how the toys move. Ask them to look carefully at the toys. (At this point, you could leave the children for a short time to allow them to explore the toys for themselves.) Then ask them to choose one which interests them and think about how it will move. Record the children's ideas on the prepared chart.

Then take each toy in turn and ask a child to make it move in some way. While the toy is moving, ask the children to describe what is happening. Questions that could be asked include:

▲ In which direction [forwards, upwards, round and round] is it moving?

▲ What do you have to hold/touch to make it move?

▲ Does more than one part move?

▲ What is the moving part called?

▲ How are the parts fitted together so that the toy can move?

▲ What material is the toy made from? Does this material help the toy to move?

(More time could be allowed for investigating the mechanisms.)

Now ask the children to choose one toy and draw it to show how the mechanism works.

Suggestion(s) for extension

The children could add labels to their drawings to explain how the mechanism works. They could research the mechanisms using books and CD-ROMs.

Suggestion(s) for support

Limit the number of toys and mechanisms shown to the children. An adult or a peer could make the toy move.

Assessment opportunities

The children's comments show their understanding of the mechanism and how it works.

Opportunities for IT

The children could create a simple database on the collection of toys, adding other toys that they have brought into school or examined at home. The database could contain such fields as:

Toy	car
Wheels	4
Mechanism	electric motor
Main material	plastic

The children could search or sort the database to find the most popular mechanism or material.

Display ideas

Make a display of toys, together with labels (drawings and/or words) for the different mechanisms. Alternatively, if it is not possible to use real toys, use pictures from catalogues and magazines.

COMING APART IDEA

To develop children's knowledge and understanding of how wheels work.

†† *Small group, working individually or in pairs.*

🕐 *30 minutes.*

⚠ *Before the activity is started, make sure the children understand that they should not take things apart unless they are given permission.*

Previous skills/knowledge needed

The wheels on vehicles are round, so that the vehicle moves smoothly along a surface. This topic is covered in chapter 6, in the 'Wheel life' activity (page 74).

Key background information

Wheels are mechanisms which help things to move. Wheels need to be able to revolve or move around a fixed point. An *axle* holds the wheel in place. The *body* of the vehicle is the shell which covers the *chassis* or *frame* around which the vehicle is built.

Language to be introduced

axle, wheel, axle holder, body, frame , chassis (if appropriate), mechanism

Preparation

Make a collection of toy vehicles (at least one for each pair of children) with wheels and axles, some of which can be taken apart and fitted together. It may be necessary to make some model vehicles using construction kits. Make a vehicle body from a box and glue four wheels on to it so that they cannot move.

Resources needed

A collection of wheeled toy vehicles, a box with wheels stuck on the side, paper and pencils.

What to do

Give each of the children a wheeled toy vehicle and ask them to look at it closely. Ask them:

▲ How many wheels does it have?

▲ What shape are the wheels?

Now ask them to make the vehicle move on the floor or the desk in front of them. Ask them what happened to the wheels when the car moved. Then ask them to look closely at the wheels and to see how they are fixed onto the car. Discuss the need for the axles and the axle holders. Ask what would happen if the wheels were stuck onto the sides of the wheeled vehicle, so that the wheels could not move. Show them the body with the wheels stuck on. The children need to understand that when the wheels cannot go round, the vehicle cannot move (except by sliding or bouncing).

Now ask the children to take their model apart and count the number of wheels and axles. If their car has a chassis and/or a body, name these parts. Give each child a sheet of paper and ask them to draw the separate parts that made up their vehicle in the top half of the sheet. When they have done this, ask them to put the vehicle together again and then to draw the completed vehicle in the bottom half of the same sheet. Encourage them to label both drawings.

Suggestion(s) for extension

Carry out the disassembly activity using different mechanisms, such as pulley wheels.

If the children have not seen a chassis, show them one that you have made from a construction kit or from construction materials, and ask them to make a vehicle with a chassis using construction kits. (Figure 2 shows a typical chassis.)

Figure 2

Suggestion(s) for support

Pair more able with less able children, so that one child can offer manipulative help if necessary.

Assessment opportunities

Through discussion, the children will show the understanding that they have about how wheels and axles work, and their knowledge of the appropriate vocabulary. Their drawings will provide opportunities to assess their drawing skills and their understanding of how the wheels and axles work.

Opportunities for IT

The children could use a simple art or drawing package to draw pictures of the wheeled vehicles. They can be shown how to use the circle command for the wheels and other drawing commands for the chassis.

Display ideas

Display the children's drawings together with the toy/model vehicles.

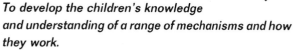

WHICH MECHANISM? ◆IDEA

To develop the children's knowledge and understanding of a range of mechanisms and how they work.

†† *Class or large group.*

🕐 *30–45 minutes.*

Previous skills/knowledge needed

Links can be made with the children's other experiences of mechanisms.

Key background information

There are different types of mechanisms, which work and move in different ways.

Language to be introduced

movement, mechanism

Specific vocabulary depends on the mechanisms displayed in the cards.

Preparation

Collect cards (from shops, or ones that children or staff have received) that have a variety of moving parts. It may be necessary to make some cards in order to provide a variety of mechanisms such as a wheel, lever, hinge, spring and slide.

Draw a chart on which to put up the cards and list the mechanisms in them. (See Figure 3.)

Resources needed

Figure 3

A collection of cards with moving parts (see above), a chart, Blu-Tack or drawing pins, one copy per child of photocopiable sheet 124.

What to do

Allow the children time to look at and investigate the movements of the cards. This can be carried out in free time during the week before the activity, or at the start of the activity while the other groups are being settled. Take each card in turn and discuss with the children how the parts move and the name of the mechanism. Then put the card up on the chart and draw and/or write the name of the mechanism beside it. Now take each card and discuss with the children whether the mechanism is suitable for the purpose. For example, if something needs to open and shut or go round and round, do the mechanisms work correctly? Ask the children:

▲ what the movement needs to be (for example, up and down, side to side);

▲ to think of a different mechanism which could have been used;

▲ to think whether a different mechanism would have been better for this movement.

Now give the children a copy each of photocopiable sheet 124 and ask them to indicate which mechanism they think would be most appropriate for each of the first three cards drawn on the sheet. Can they invent a mechanism for the fourth card?

Suggestion(s) for extension

Using books and CD-ROMs, the children could research further into mechanisms and create their own factual books about them. Encourage the children to bring in greetings cards that have moving parts of various kinds, and to ask each other about how the visible movements are achieved.

Ask the children to look for the mechanisms that they have seen in the cards in things they see or use in their everyday lives.

Suggestion(s) for support

Some children may need help to decide which mechanism on the photocopiable sheet to choose for each card. Further discussion about what type of movement is needed in the cards may be necessary.

Assessment opportunities

During the discussion and the completion of the photocopiable sheet, the children will show whether they have an understanding of the word *mechanism* and of how different mechanisms work.

Display ideas

Display a collection of cards with moving parts. Put up questions around the cards, such as: *What mechanisms can you see? What movements can you see? Can you see something that moves up and down? Can you see something that moves round and round?*

Reference to photocopiable sheet

Ask the children to indicate which mechanism will make the right movement for each of the first three cards. The last card on the sheet is an extension to see if they can devise their own mechanism.

RAISE THE PRESSURE ◆IDEA

To develop the children's knowledge and understanding of the use of air to transmit force, and how air pressure can be harnessed to make things move.

✝✝ *Class working in small groups, or a small group.*

🕐 *30 minutes.*

⚠ *Only syringes bought for the purpose should be used. Different children should not blow down the same piece of tubing unless it has been sterilised in between.*

Previous skills/knowledge needed

Air is all around us.

Key background information

Air can be harnessed and controlled so that it can be used to move things. This activity could be used as an introduction to 'Open and shut' (page 36).

Language to be introduced

air, pneumatic, syringe, tubing, plunger

Preparation

Make the models shown in Figure 4. Make sure that there are enough models for each group to work with two.

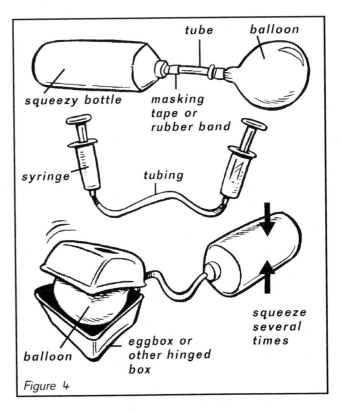

Figure 4

Resources needed

Large sheet of paper for class/group list, sterilising liquid, models (see above), one copy per child of photocopiable sheet 125.

What to do

Ask two or three children to blow up balloons and let them go. Watch what happens to them. Ask the children what was inside the balloons and why they think that the balloons shoot around the room before falling to the ground. Explain that it is possible to use air to make things move in the way that you want.

Show them the balloon attached to the tube and the squeezy bottle. Press the bottle several times and watch what happens to the balloon. Now put the balloon into the egg-box, squeeze the bottle and see the lid lift. (If the balloon does not expand much, you could adapt the model as shown in Figure 5.)

Figure 5

Show the children the two syringes attached to a piece of tubing (as shown in Figure 4). Ask what is inside the tubing and the syringes. Now ask the children to predict what will happen when the plunger in one syringe is pushed down. Test their predictions.

Ask the children whether they know of any ways that air is used to move things in their everyday lives. Examples might include pneumatic drills, car jacks and brake systems on goods vehicles. Start to make a class/group list, which can be added to later. Allow the children time to investigate on their own and to fill in their own copies of photocopiable sheet 125. Talk about their findings at the end of the activity.

Suggestion(s) for extension

Ask the children to research (using, for example, books and CD-ROMs) what machines or mechanisms use air to make something move. They can add their findings to the list.

Suggestion(s) for support

Children may need help to push the squeezy bottle or blow up the balloon. They may need help to fill in the photocopiable sheet, perhaps in the form of two or three alternative answers to each question.

Assessment opportunities

Listen to the children's comments about what is in the balloon and how air can be used to move things. The children's answers on the photocopiable sheet will indicate whether they have an understanding of how air can be used mechanically.

Opportunities for IT

The children could use an encyclopaedic CD-ROM to research other mechanisms that work by air. They may need to be given other key words, such as *pneumatic*, to help them search.

Display ideas

Display the syringes and tubing and the balloon, tubing and box. Enlarge a few of the completed photocopiable sheets to mount beside the models. Put up questions for the children to investigate, such as: *What happens when the balloon is blown up? What happens when you push the plunger down?* Display the list of things which use air to make them work, along with pictures or small models.

Reference to photocopiable sheet

Photocopiable sheet 125 asks the children to predict (and draw) the effect of each of the actions shown.

ROUND AND ROUND · FPT

To develop knowledge and understanding of wheels and axles.

†† *Small group; children can work in pairs.*

🕑 *45–60 minutes.*

Previous skills/knowledge needed
The children should have experienced the work outlined in the IDEA 'Coming apart' (page 27), relating to wheels. They will need cutting skills.

Key background information
To allow wheels to turn round smoothly, they can be attached to axles which are held onto the vehicle by axle holders. Either the axles or the wheels can turn. If they both turn independently, the vehicle will not move in a controllable way.

Language to be introduced
axle, wheel, axle holder, body, mechanism

Preparation
Turn the boxes that the children will use inside-out and tape them together using masking tape (optional). This will provide the children with a plain box which can be decorated at a later time, giving a clean surface to which they can add a quality finish.

Make two vehicle bodies from cardboard boxes and put axle holders on one. Fix the holders with masking tape, so that their position on the box can be changed easily. (See Figure 6.)

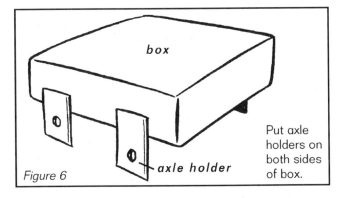

box

axle holder

Put axle holders on both sides of box.

Figure 6

Resources needed
Cardboard boxes, masking tape, tubing, straws, cotton reels (card or wood wheels could be used), card, scissors, Plasticine, solid glue stick, paper fasteners.

What to do
Display the materials so that the children can see them. Explain to the children that they are going to fix wheels onto the body of a vehicle so that the vehicle can move. Show the children the body of the vehicle and ask for their ideas as to how to fix the wheels (card or wood wheels or cotton reels) to the vehicle with the equipment that you have on display. Try out some of their ideas, asking for comments on the advantages and the disadvantages of each method. If there are no ideas forthcoming or the ideas are not suitable, talk about the three methods outlined in Figure 7.

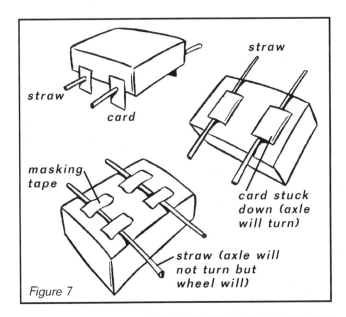

straw

straw

card

masking tape

card stuck down (axle will turn)

straw (axle will not turn but wheel will)

Figure 7

Ask the children to think about what would happen if the axles were in different places on different sides of the body. Show them an example (see Figure 8), and demonstrate that it will not go straight. Emphasise how important it is to measure and mark the places where the axles need to go.

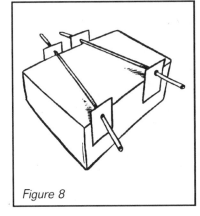

Figure 8

Then ask the children to suggest how they can secure the wheels onto the axles, using the equipment that is on display. If it is practical, let them try out other ideas. If they have no suitable ideas, show the children the ways outlined in Figure 9.

Now ask the children to choose a body for the vehicle from the boxes already prepared for them. Ask them to decide how they will fix the axles onto the body and then fix the wheels onto the axles. Allow the children time to fix their wheels. At the end of the task, ask them:

▲ Are the axles fixed firmly to the body?

▲ Do the wheels go round freely?

▲ Do the wheels stay on?

▲ What problems did you encounter?

▲ Would you choose a different way of doing it next time? If so, why?

DESIGN AND TECHNOLOGY

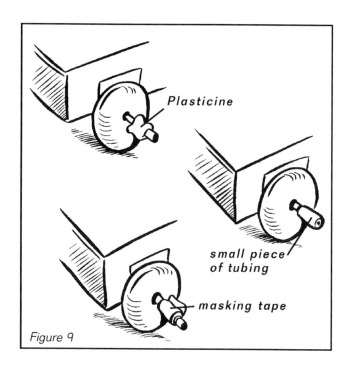

Plasticine

small piece of tubing

masking tape

Figure 9

Ask the children to draw their finished vehicle and add labels if appropriate. They could decorate their vehicles now or at a later date.

Suggestion(s) for extension

The children could investigate what happens when they use wheels which are not round.

They could write up a report on how they fixed their wheels, including any changes they would make next time.

Suggestion(s) for support

Put the children into appropriate pairs, so that more able children can support less able ones. Help may be needed to push the plastic tubing onto the axle. It may be necessary to check that the children have measured the positions of the axles accurately.

Assessment opportunities

From their finished models and the discussion, it will be possible to see those children who:
▲ understand that wheels need to turn round and that axles help them to do this;
▲ can measure accurately, make joins and select appropriate materials to finish the task.

Opportunities for IT

The children could use a word processor to write a report on how they have made their vehicle. Older or more able children could also use an art or drawing package to draw a picture of their vehicle, which could be added to their written report.

Display ideas

Display the finished vehicles, together with the children's written reports about how they fixed their wheels.

MOVING ON UP   FPT

To develop the children's knowledge and understanding of how different mechanisms work. To develop the children's ability to make different mechanisms.

†† *Small group.*

⏱ *60 minutes. (The last part of the task could be carried out at a different time.)*

Previous skills/knowledge needed

The children will need cutting skills. They can make links with other knowledge about mechanisms, such as that gained from the activity 'Make a move' (page 26).

Key background information

Different types of mechanism work and move in different ways.

A **slide** mechanism allows movement up and down or from side to side; it is often used to open or close something. Examples include a hair slide and a bolt on a door.

A **lever** mechanism moves things up and down or back and forth. There are different classes of lever; the example given in this chapter is a first order lever. It is a bar which is pivoted about a fulcrum or axis and is used to lift something. Examples include a claw hammer, a spade and a seesaw.

A **hinge** mechanism is a joint which allows movement in one plane. Examples include the hinges on doors, spectacles, bivalved shells and purses.

Language to be introduced

mechanism, movement, lever, slide, hinge, flap

Preparation

Prepare examples of each mechanism shown in Figures 10, 11 and 12, enough for one between two children. Copy photocopiable sheet 126 onto card.

Resources needed

Examples of mechanisms (see above), scissors, paper fasteners, Pritt stick, paper for hinges, one copy per child of photocopiable sheet 126 (on card), blank paper, pencils.

What to do

This activity can be carried out a number of times, using a different mechanism each time.

For each task, tell the children that they are going to look at the mechanism and then make one themselves. Show the children how each mechanism works and tell them its name.

Task 1: A slide

Show the children how the slide moves from side to side or up and down. When the children make their own, show them how to cut slits in the card. (See Figure 10.)

DESIGN AND TECHNOLOGY

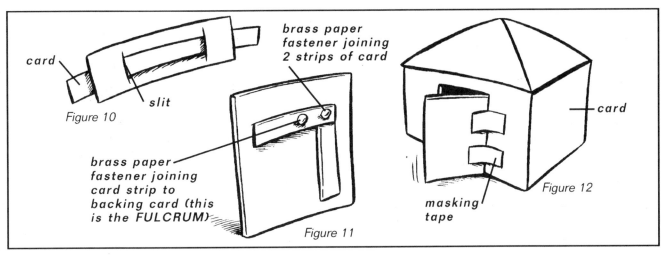

card

slit

Figure 10

brass paper fastener joining card strip to backing card (this is the FULCRUM)

brass paper fastener joining 2 strips of card

Figure 11

card

Figure 12

masking tape

Task 2: A lever
Change the position of the fastener and see how the movement changes: the nearer the fulcrum, the greater the movement. (See Figure 11.)

Task 3: A hinge
Show the children how to attach the door to the house by the hinges. (See Figure 12.)

Talk about the uses of slides, levers and hinges in everyday life. Now give the children examples of mechanisms which have been prepared, and give them time to investigate these. While they are doing this, ask questions such as:
▲ How does it move?
▲ What direction does it move in?
▲ What do you need to make the mechanism?
▲ Can you think of things in the classroom or at home which have this mechanism?

Review what the children have found out. Then ask them to make up the mechanisms using photocopiable sheet 126, and to add appropriate pictures as background. Ask them to draw one of their mechanisms from the front and the back view on a blank sheet of paper, and to add labels where appropriate. (This part of the task could be carried out later.)

Suggestion(s) for extension
Let the children design and make their own mechanisms using card, reclaimed materials or construction kits, using the teacher's models as a resource.

Suggestion(s) for support
Help may be needed with cutting out the shapes or fixing the fastener in place.

Assessment opportunities
During the discussion, note which children have an understanding of the mechanism and how it moves. The children's models will give an indication of their ability to cut, join and assemble a mechanism.

Opportunities for IT
The children could use a word processor or desk-top publishing package to make labels for a display of their mechanisms. They should be shown how to select the size of the fonts to make their work readable from a distance.

Display ideas
Make a display of some models of each of the mechanisms. The children can make labels using a word processing or DTP program. Add objects which have these mechanisms on display.

Reference to photocopiable sheets
Using photocopiable sheet 126, the children will need to cut out the shapes and fix them together to make the different mechanism for each task. They can then add a picture of their own, perhaps choosing to put it in a context. Using a blank sheet of paper, the children will then draw both the back and the front view of one of their mechanisms.

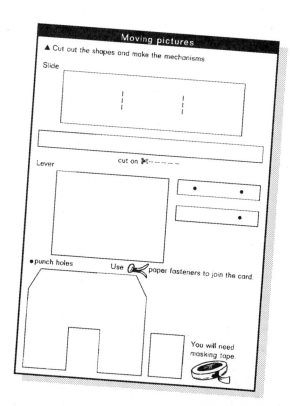

ANYONE CAN JOIN ◆FPT

To develop the children's understanding of how moving joints work. To develop the children's ability to join pieces of card.

†† *Class or large group.*

⏱ *60 minutes.*

⚠ *Check that the children know how to hold and use scissors safely, particularly if they are going to move around the room with scissors in their hands. All work with scissors must be closely supervised.*

Previous skills/knowledge needed

It will be helpful if the children have an understanding of joints in, for example, the human body. They should know how to use a hole punch.

Key background information

Two parts can be joined together in a way that allows relative movement. This is called a joint. We have joints in our bodies, and there are joints in many everyday objects. Joints can allow movement in a number of directions.

Language to be introduced

joints, hole punch, join, tag, paper fastener, string, elastic

Preparation

Make up a collection of materials used for joining, such as masking tape, elastic, wool/string, paper fasteners, treasury tags, solid glue sticks and paper clips. Include some that will allow the joint to move and others that will not. Copy photocopiable sheet 127 onto card. Cut out one clown, ready to use with the children. Check that there are enough pairs of scissors available.

Resources needed

A selection of items for joining card, a hole punch, scissors, colouring equipment, one copy per child of photocopiable sheet 127.

What to do

Ask the children to move their hands up and down. Talk to them about how the hand moves, and introduce the word *joint*. Ask them to try bending their arm at the elbow, and ask if they know what helps them to do this. Ask them if they have any other joints in their bodies.

Now show them the clown figure which you have already cut out. Lay out the pre-cut shapes. Explain to the children that they are going to try different ways of joining the parts to make a clown for themselves – but first, they need to make holes in the shapes. Show the children how the hole punch works and let them try it out on scraps of cards. Then show them the collection of things that they can use for

joining. Take each one in turn, name it and show the children how it works. Compare the different methods.

Give the children each a copy of photocopiable sheet 127 and explain that they are to cut out the body parts and join them together to make their own clown. Using a hole punch, they should make holes where there are small circles on the parts of the clown. While the children are working, talk with them about the different methods of joining and which work best. The children can colour in the clown when it is joined together. At the end of the activity, look at the different methods that the children have used to join the arms and legs to the body. Do their joints move? Which methods do they think work well? Which do they think are not so effective?

Suggestion(s) for extension

The children could repeat the task, this time joining reclaimed materials such as cardboard boxes, cylindrical rolls and egg boxes to make a fantasy person or animal. The joints can then move back and forth or round and round, as well as from side to side.

Suggestion(s) for support

Help may be needed with cutting out the shapes, punching the holes or fixing the joints.

Assessment opportunities

Through their discussion and their use of the different joints in the clown, the children will show their knowledge and understanding of the types of joint and their ability to select and use them.

Opportunities for IT

The children might design and colour their own clown, using an art package. This design could then be printed out, stuck on card and cut out to make a clown with moving parts.

Display ideas

Make a display of the different joints and/or the finished clowns. Make a display of the different joints on one life-sized clown.

Reference to photocopiable sheet

The children need to cut out the different shapes on photocopiable sheet 127. They can then choose how to join the arms and legs to the body using different joining materials. They should use things that will allow the joint to move from side to side.

WOUND UP   FPT

To develop the children's understanding of how pulley wheels and winding mechanisms can be used to help lift heavy loads. To develop the children's making skills.

†† *Small group.*

🕐 *45–60 minutes.*

Previous skills/knowledge needed

It will be useful if the children are able to cut with scissors and/or snips, make holes and saw pieces of dowel.

Key background information

A pulley wheel always has a groove to stop the rope (or wire, or string) slipping off. Because the pulley wheel turns round, it makes it easier for someone to lift a heavy load. The winding mechanism helps someone to turn the axle and wind up the heavy object. The rope is wound round the pulley wheel.

Language to be introduced

winding, mechanism, pulley, wheel, lift, groove

Preparation

Find a copy of the nursery rhyme 'Ding dong bell, Pussy's in the well'. Make an example of a winding mechanism, as shown in Figure 13. Collect the materials and tools listed in 'Resources needed'.

Resources needed

A copy of the rhyme 'Pussy's in the well', hole punches, scissors, string, wool, boxes, cotton reels, straws, dowel, snips, junior bench hooks, junior hacksaws, G-clamps (one for each group). Materials to decorate the finished model, such as paints, crayons and a variety of types of paper.

What to do

Read out the nursery rhyme 'Pussy's in the well'. Ask the children how they think Johnny Stout got the cat out. Then show them the examples of pulley wheels and winding mechanisms and demonstrate how they work. Talk about how they have been made and what they could be made into. Tell them that the wheel is called a *pulley wheel*.

Explain that they are going to use a pulley wheel and winding mechanism and ask them to draw what they are going to make, using the models to help them. During the making process, give help when required. Check that the children are measuring where they are to punch their holes and fix their wheels. Ask the children how their model works, what they did easily and what changes they would make another time. Explain to the children that they can finish the model by decorating it.

Suggestion(s) for extension

The children could make another model, using different materials and a different context. Ideas could include making something that the Little Red Hen could use to help her get the sacks of grain into the mill, or something to help the spider go up and down the water spout.

Suggestion(s) for support

Help may be needed with punching holes, cutting and sticking the wheels in place. Construction kits could be used instead of reclaimed materials.

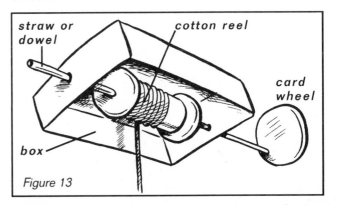

Figure 13

Assessment opportunities

From discussion with the children, it will be possible to assess their understanding of the use of pulley wheels and winding mechanisms and their ability to evaluate their own product. From the finished model, it will be possible to assess their measuring, cutting, hole punching and finishing skills.

Opportunities for IT

The children could use a word processor or desktop publishing package to make labels for a display of their pulleys. They could also use an art package to make pictures of how pulleys are used in everyday life, or a CD-ROM to research information about pulleys.

Display ideas

Display the models together with pictures of objects in everyday life that contain pulley wheels and winding mechanisms.

OPEN AND SHUT ◇ FPT

To develop the children's understanding of pneumatic forces. To develop the children's making skills. To develop the children's ability to work co-operatively.

†† *Small group, working in pairs.*

⏲ *45–60 minutes.*

Previous skills/knowledge needed

The children need the knowledge gained through the IDEA 'Raise the pressure' on page 29.

Key background information

Air is a material which can exert (or transmit) a force. This force can be used to lift and move objects.

When making their model, the children need to think about the best place for the balloon. If it is too near the hinge joint or fulcrum, it will be difficult to move but there will be more movement. Further away, it will be easier to move but there will be less movement.

Language to be introduced

air, pneumatic, balloon, squeezy bottle, tubing, force

Preparation

Make a model using a squeezy bottle and balloon (see Figure 14). Check that there are enough squeezy bottles and balloons, one for each pair. Cut lengths of tubing, approximately 20cm. Create access to items that the children can use to decorate their models, such as paints, felt-tipped pens, tissue paper and solid glue stick.

Resources needed

Squeezy bottles, tubing, rubber bands, masking tape, egg boxes, balloons, decorating materials (see above).

What to do

Explain to the children that they are going to make a mouth that opens and shuts. Put out the model and ask the children to watch carefully what happens. Ask them how the box can open. Blow up the balloon and watch what happens. Now ask the children which is the best position for the balloon, near the front or near the hinge. Try both ways and talk about what happens.

Now examine how the model is made. Talk about how the different parts are fitted together. Tell the children that they can make their own working model of a mouth and decorate it. They will need to think what mouth they are going to make: a monster, a dragon, a lion? Offer help with making when needed, and encourage the children to work and make decisions together. When the models are finished, ask the children to say whether their model opens and shuts, what difficulties they had and how they overcame them.

Suggestion(s) for extension

Children could make various models, such as a treasure box or a jack-in-the-box, using boxes, and pneumatic mechanisms. Instead of balloons, they could use tubing and syringes to make their models move.

Suggestion(s) for support

Children may need help fixing the tubing to the balloon.

Assessment opportunities

During discussions with the children, it will be possible to assess their understanding of how air is used to move things. From their making task, it will be possible to assess how well they can select appropriate materials, join parts together and finish a model.

Display ideas

Display the children's models together with large labelled drawings of the different parts that have been used.

Display pictures of objects in our everyday lives which use pneumatic forces.

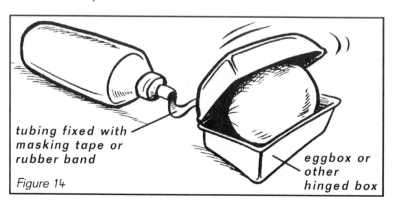

tubing fixed with masking tape or rubber band

Figure 14

eggbox or other hinged box

DESIGN AND TECHNOLOGY

Reclaimed materials

Much has been said about the problems of working with reclaimed materials, particularly in relation to the making of a quality product. It has been argued that children working with 'junk' materials can only make 'junk' products! This need not be the case. If the children are provided with a carefully sorted selection of reclaimed materials, together with appropriate joiners, it is possible for them to produce good quality models.

Through the activities in this chapter, children will have the opportunity to develop skills including discussing and modelling ideas and exploring and investigating a range of reclaimed materials. The making skills developed through these activities include selecting appropriate materials and tools, joining materials using a variety of materials and techniques and evaluating their own products. The children are also given opportunities to investigate, disassemble and evaluate a variety of reclaimed materials, looking at the strength of different materials. They should also learn about the need to work safely and the safe handling of tools, as well as the importance of using the correct technical vocabulary.

The following contexts are appropriate for work with reclaimed materials: shops and shopping, houses and homes, animals, ourselves, transport, the playground, materials.

⚠ It is important that the glue gun is used correctly, and that glues or adhesives used are not solvent-based.

DESIGN AND
TECHNOLOGY

SORTING MATERIALS ◆IDEA

To develop the children's ability to sort materials against various criteria.

†† *Large or small group.*

🕐 *30–45 minutes.*

Key background information
Part of the children's ability to use reclaimed materials in appropriate ways is based on their knowledge about what materials they were made from.

Language to be introduced
reclaimed material, plastic, flexible, hard, inflexible, card, paper, criteria, sort, set

Preparation
Make a collection of reclaimed materials for each group that contains a variety of types of material, including ones that are the same but look different (such as different types of paper and card).

Resources needed
Three hoops per group, a collection of reclaimed materials, writing materials, one copy per child of the sorting photocopiable sheet (page 128).

What to do
Lay out the reclaimed materials on the floor or table so that all the children can see them clearly. Give each group a short time to examine them, and tell them to find out what material they are made from. First ask the children to find items made from, for example, card, paper or plastic before they begin sorting. Then suggest that the children sort the materials into two groups, using criteria such as:

▲ card/not card;

▲ plastic/not plastic;

▲ paper/not paper.

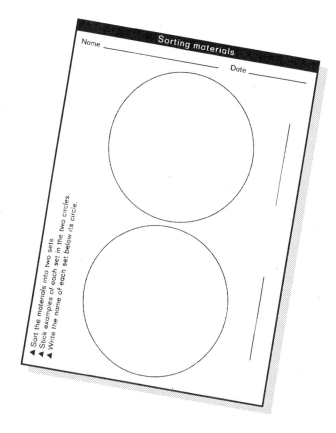

When they finish sorting, check with them what they have done and discuss any items they were unsure about. Give the children time to choose their own criteria and sort the materials again. Finally, ask the children to choose one of the criteria, sort the materials and record their findings by drawing and/or writing on photocopiable sheet 128.

Suggestion(s) for extension
The children can sort using overlapping sets, such as items which are made from card, plastic or card and plastic.

Suggestion(s) for support
The children may need help to sort and to choose their own criteria for sorting.

DESIGN AND TECHNOLOGY

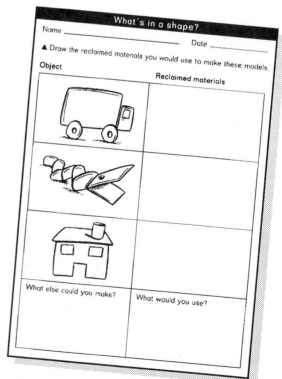

Assessment opportunities

From watching the children sort, it will be possible to determine those children who understand how to sort and can identify a range of materials.

Display ideas

Display different sets of reclaimed materials and change them at regular intervals. Ask the children to make the labels using a word processing or DTP program.

Reference to photocopiable sheet

Ask the children to record their sorting activity on photocopiable sheet 128. They could be encouraged to add a central (overlapping) circle of their own if appropriate. Ask them to fill in the name of the material at the bottom of the sheet, for example:

card   not card

LOOKING AT SHAPES   ◆ IDEA

To investigate the shapes of a range of reclaimed materials. To model ideas.

†† *Large group or small group.*

🕐 *30–45 minutes.*

Previous skills/knowledge needed

The activity can be related to any other experiences relating to sorting and shape, that the children have had.

Key background information

Before constructing with materials, the children need to be able to recognise different shapes and sizes and relate these to the shapes and sizes needed for their construction.

Language to be introduced

shape, size, reclaimed material, thick, thin, wide, narrow, square, rectangular, circular, triangular

Preparation

Collect together a range of reclaimed materials, making sure that there is a variety of materials, shapes and sizes; include boxes, cylindrical rolls and plastic tubs. Put out masking tape and Blu-Tack.

Resources needed

Collection of reclaimed materials, Blu-Tack, masking tape, scissors, one copy per child of photocopiable sheet 129.

What to do

Put out the collection of materials so that the children can see them. Ask the children to look at them carefully. Get them to sort the materials initially using criteria relating to

shape. Then ask them to suggest ways of sorting.

Hold up selected items one at a time. Ask the children: if you were going to make a model, what could you use this object for? Alternatively, the question could be put the other way round: if you are going to make a bus, which is the best-shaped object for this? Other suggestions for objects to make could include different vehicles, houses, playground or fairground equipment, a mouth, a tail and the body of a person or animal. Encourage the children to talk about what they could make and why they would choose a particular object.

At the end of the discussion, ask the children to fill in photocopiable sheet 129. The children will need to have the materials in front of them while filling in the sheet. Ask them to draw what they would use to make the models in the three pictures. In the final part of the sheet, they have to draw something they could make and whichever reclaimed materials they would make it with.

DESIGN AND TECHNOLOGY

Suggestion(s) for extension

The children could try building one of the models on the photocopiable sheet, fixing the items together with Blu-Tack or masking tape.

Suggestion(s) for support

The children may need first to be given ideas of things to make before they can think for themselves about the use of the materials (especially if they have forgotten the suggestions made earlier on). Some children may need assistance to fill in the final boxes on the photocopiable sheet.

Assessment opportunities

From the children's comments and their work on photocopiable sheet 129, it will be possible to assess whether they can match the shapes of the reclaimed materials to models that they may want to make or objects in their everyday lives.

Opportunities for IT

The children could use a simple drawing or art package to create a design for a model made from reclaimed materials. Framework software such as 'My World 2' with a suitable shape file could be used for a similar activity.

Display ideas

The children can display the reclaimed materials alongside their design drawings or computer pictures of what the shapes could be made into.

Reference to photocopiable sheet

Photocopiable sheet 129 asks children to choose appropriate reclaimed materials (from a collection) to make models of specified objects.

TAKING A BOX APART

To investigate, disassemble and reassemble a box. To work together co-operatively.
†† *Large or small group; opportunity for pair work.*
🕐 *45–60 minutes.*

Key background information

Cardboard boxes are not usually made from a number of separate pieces of card joined together: they are usually made from a single flat piece of card folded up. When boxes are taken apart and flattened, it is possible to see the original shape from which they were made. This shape is called a *net*.

Language to be introduced

box, shape, net, join, fold, flap, seam

Preparation

Make a collection of boxes of different shapes and sizes, such as cereal, tissue, chocolate and shoe boxes.

Resources needed

A collection of cardboard boxes, masking tape, scissors.

What to do

Show the children a cardboard box and ask them for their ideas about how the box is made up. They may suggest that there are lots of pieces of card stuck together, or they may know about nets from work in mathematics. Ask the children to find out whether their ideas were right by opening out a box. Alternatively, you could give out boxes (one between three or four children) and ask the children to look at them closely. Can they see anything which helps them to find out how the box is made up? They may suggest that there is a seam or join which they can undo. Undo the seam and let the children open out the box and flatten it. Ask questions such as:

▲ What shapes can you see?
▲ How were the flaps and the seam made?
▲ How was the seam fastened when the box was made up?

When the children have explored the net, ask them to reassemble the box, with the original inside on the outside. This will give them practice at turning boxes inside-out for modelling. (If plain card surfaces are visible, they can decorate these surfaces more easily.) Emphasise the need to press along the folds as they reassemble the net. The children can work in pairs, each child having a box. They will need to work together when they put masking tape along the seam to hold it together. Check that they cut the tape with scissors (not teeth) for safety and for a quality finish. When the boxes have been reassembled successfully, they can be kept for use in another activity.

A POPULAR PACKAGE ◆IDEA

To investigate and evaluate the features which make packaging attractive. To design an attractive exterior for a package.

†† *Large or small group.*

⏱ *45–60 minutes.*

Key background information

It is important that the children understand why different shapes, types of lettering, drawings and pictures are used to advertise goods. People have different needs, preferences and uses for products, and manufacturers want to sell to as many people as possible. The children need to be aware of this, and to realise and accept that others' opinions may differ from their own.

Language to be introduced

bright, eye-catching, advertising, colours, lettering, picture, photograph, bold, slogan, attractive, packet

Preparation

Collect packaging for different types of products, with different colours and types of lettering. Put all the packaging in a large bag, so that the children cannot see it. Turn some cardboard boxes inside-out, one for each child – or use ones that have already been turned inside-out in the 'Taking a box apart' activity (page 40).

Resources needed

A collection of packaging, a collection of packaging turned inside-out, a chart or flip chart, felt-tipped pens, crayons, paints, paper, drawing materials.

What to do

Explain to the children that you have several different packages, and that you want them to tell you which one they think is the most eye-catching. Ask them to shut their eyes while you pull out the packages. Then tell them to look very quickly at all of the boxes and to decide which one they think looks most attractive and why. Give them five seconds, then take the boxes away and ask for their choices. Explain to the children that they did not have much time to see the packets because you wanted to see which ones 'caught their eye'. Make a list of the children's choices and the reasons for them on a chart or flip chart, as in Figure 1.

Suggestion(s) for extension

The children could add a finish to the box to make it into a more useful and/or decorative artefact. They could draw and cut out their own net and make it up into a box, then decide on a purpose for the box and decorate it accordingly.

Other types of reclaimed material, such as egg boxes and cylindrical tubes, could be investigated, disassembled and reassembled in the same way.

Suggestion(s) for support

Some children may need help to open the box along the seam, reassemble the box and close it with masking tape.

Assessment opportunities

The comments that the children make while disassembling and reassembling the boxes will indicate whether they have an understanding of nets.

Opportunities for IT

The children could use a simple shape or drawing program to create a net for a box. It often helps if a drawing package is used to turn on the background grid, which will help the children to draw straight lines of the same length. The 'lock to grid' option is also useful, as it helps to ensure that the lines will meet up accurately with the points on the background grid.

Display ideas

Make a display using three boxes which were initially the same. Put up one as it is, one as a net and one which has been turned inside-out. Add large labels to explain the display.

Display a variety of boxes and their nets, with the question *Can you match the net with the box?* written alongside.

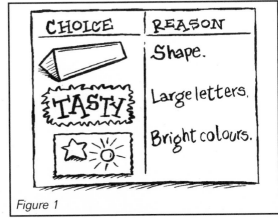

Figure 1

DESIGN AND TECHNOLOGY

Now put out the packets again. Ask the children to look at different aspects of the packets: the lettering, the colours, the words and slogans, the pictures and where things are placed on the packet. Discuss with them why these have been used and whether each packet 'looks good'. Encourage the children to express different opinions, helping them to appreciate that different people have different preferences and that we should respect other people's opinions.

Now explain that they are going to make their own design for a box. Give each child a plain box. Ask the children to draw a design for their box on paper – thinking about what is inside, the use of colours, lettering and pictures. Talk with the children while they are doing this and ask appropriate questions. Encourage them to ask each other for their opinions and ideas. When the children have a design with which they are satisfied, let them copy it onto their box. Remind them of the importance of a quality finish. (The children could transfer their designs to the boxes at a different time.)

Suggestion(s) for extension
The children could choose their favourite package and write up a report on the reasons for their choice.

Suggestion(s) for support
Some children may need help to decide what product would be in their box. Some may need help with lettering.

Assessment opportunities
From watching the children make choices, listening to the reason for their choices and looking at their finished packages, it will be possible to assess their understanding of the importance of an eye-catching appearance when creating packaging and their ability to produce a quality finish.

Opportunities for IT
The children could use a word processor or desktop publishing package to create the lettering for their packaging. They will need to be shown how to select an appropriate font and change its size (and possibly its colour as well). Pictures could be added to create a full design. The children could scan in their own line drawings, or use pictures taken from a suitable clipart.

Alternatively, the children could use an art or drawing package to create the design. They could use the software to draw the pictures and the text facilities to add the appropriate lettering. Using a graphics package gives more varied possibilities for positioning the text on the page, and even shaping it to make it look more interesting.

Display ideas
Display the children's finished packages. Put up questions such as: *Which is the brightest? Which have a quality finish? Which do you like best? Why? Which ones show you what is inside?* Real packets could be added. The question *What are the differences and similarities?* could be displayed.

MAKING A HINGE   FPT

To know what a hinge is. To make a hinge in a variety of ways, using a variety of joiners. To develop co-operative working skills.

†† *Class; large group; small group.*

⏱ *45–60 minutes.*

Previous skills/knowledge needed
The children should be able to use a range of joiners, such as brass paper fasteners, glue, tags, string, masking tape, elastic and a hole puncher, and be able to tie a knot.

Key background information
Reclaimed materials can be joined in a number of ways, depending on the material from which they are made and the joining materials that are available. A hinge is something which joins things together and allows relative movement in one dimension only. It is thus a type of joint (see 'Anyone can join', page 34).

DESIGN AND TECHNOLOGY

Language to be introduced
join, hinge, tags, elastic, masking tape, fabric, glue, spreader, string, paper fastener, pipe cleaner

Preparation
Collect various items (see 'Resources needed') that the children could use to make hinges. Cut the hinges on egg boxes or cut small boxes in two, so that each child has two pieces to start with. Have more ready for any early finishers. As an example for the children, join one egg box to make a hinge.

Resources needed
A model with a hinge, treasury tags, paper fasteners, fabric, elastic, glue and spreaders, pipe cleaners, masking tape, string, scissors, hole punchers, egg boxes, small boxes, paper and pencils.

What to do
Explain to the children that they are going to find out different ways of joining materials to can make hinges. Show the children a model with a hinge and ask them which objects in the room might have hinges. Discuss why a hinge is useful, before showing the children which items they can use to join different materials. Discuss with the children different ways of joining the boxes before they try it for themselves. Then let each group find different ways of joining things to make hinges. Each child should complete two ways at least. (Figure 2 shows some possible ways.) Encourage the children to talk with, and help, each other.

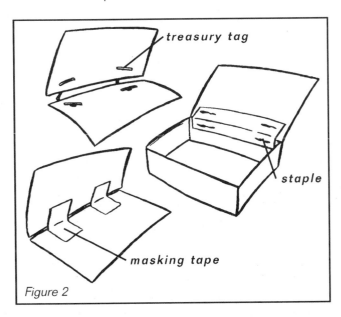

treasury tag

staple

masking tape

Figure 2

As a final discussion, ask the children to explain to each to other what they have used, how the hinge works and what difficulties they experienced when they were making the hinge. Finally, ask the children to draw some different ways of making a hinge on a sheet of paper. Encourage them to label their drawings to show which materials they have used.

Suggestion(s) for extension
Encourage the children to make something with the materials that they have joined together. They could use hinged boxes to make the face of a person or monster, or a container for a precious jewel.

Suggestion(s) for support
Some children may need help to use some of the joiners successfully.

Assessment opportunities
From the comments that the children make and their recording on blank paper, it will be possible to assess their understanding of joiners and hinges.

Display ideas
Display each group's ways of making hinges. Encourage the children to arrange their work in an interesting way and add labels to it.

DESIGN AND TECHNOLOGY

HOW STRONG IS IT? ◆IDEA

To investigate how well different structures withstand different loads.

†† *Class or large group.*

🕐 *30–45 minutes.*

Previous skills/knowledge needed

The children need to know that the strength of a material can be changed if its shape is changed.

Key background information

Depending on the strength of a box, when a force is applied to it, it may change shape; the greater the force, the greater the change in the shape. The strength of a box depends partly on its structure. This knowledge will be needed when using boxes in construction.

Language to be introduced

structure, force, push, sag, mass, load

Preparation

Make a collection of boxes of different sizes and shapes. For the work relating to the photocopiable sheet, the children will need two identical boxes each. Collect a large amount of Plasticine (or something similar) that can be used as a mass. Plasticine is particularly useful, as its shape can be changed.

Resources needed

A collection of boxes, Plasticine, one copy per child of photocopiable sheet 130.

What to do

Hold up a box and make sure that the children can see it clearly, so that they can see the changes to it when a force is

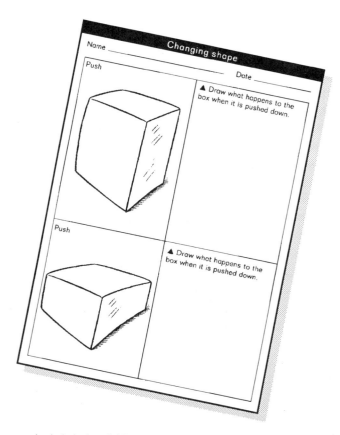

applied. Ask the children what they think might happen when a force (push) is applied to the box. Try each face of the box in turn, recording on a chart first the children's ideas and then what happens. Ask the children why they think the box bends. Ask them whether this test is fair. How could it be made fairer? Repeat the test more fairly, with the same amount of mass applied in the same place (the middle). Check whether the results are the same.

Now discuss with the children what might happen if they used the box when they were making something. Ask them whether different sides will hold a given mass without bending.

The children should begin to understand that if the same amount of force is applied to different surfaces, a wider face will bend more than a narrower face.

Finally, give the children two identical boxes each. Ask them to work in pairs and fill in photocopiable sheet 130 to show what happens when a force is applied to each side of the box.

Suggestion(s) for extension
The children could think of ways to support the large flat surfaces of a box so that it can withstand greater loads, and try these ideas out. Does the box have to be strengthened from inside, or could it be strengthened from outside? The children could devise their own fair tests and work in groups to investigate their ideas.

Suggestion(s) for support
Some children may need additional discussion about the effects of shape on strength, and may then need help to relate these ideas to the photocopiable sheet.

Assessment opportunities
Listen to the comments that the children make about the changes that happen to the box. Use their work on the photocopiable sheet to assess their understanding of how structures can withstand loads.

Display ideas
Display various boxes with a mass on one face of each, alongside some of the completed photocopiable sheets.

Reference to photocopiable sheet
Each child needs to have access to two identical boxes, so that she can try out her ideas before drawing what happens to the box when a force is applied to different faces.

JOINING A THIN SURFACE ◆ FPT

To develop joining and finishing techniques.

†† *Large or small group.*

🕐 *60 minutes.*

⚠ *Some LEAs discourage the use of toilet roll tubes. Check before using them!*

Key background information
It can be very difficult to join an object with a thin surface to another object, because the surface is hard to attach things to. There are techniques for changing the thin surface, by cutting and bending it, so that it can be joined.

Language to be introduced
join, cut, surface, thin, narrow, broad, flat, slot, flap

Preparation
Prepare three different ways of joining something with a thin surface to show the children. (See Figure 3.) Make a container or a flower, a divider and a chair. (See Figure 4.)

Collect some tubes and make sure that the other equipment needed is available. Open out a box so that the flaps can be seen.

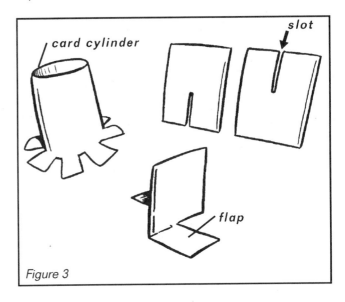

Figure 3

Figure 4

Resources needed
Cylindrical tubes, a collection of small boxes, scissors, PVA glue.

What to do
Take a box with flaps at the end, and discuss with the children how the flaps could be used to join the box to another surface. Emphasise the fact that only a little glue is needed, and it must be spread evenly over the surface. Then take something with a very thin surface, such as a cylindrical tube, and ask the children if they can think of ways of joining this to another surface. Suggestions might include cutting slits in the bottom

DESIGN AND TECHNOLOGY

Opportunities for IT

The children could use a word processor to write a sequence of instructions for joining thin surfaces. They could use the 'cut and paste' or 'drag and drop' facility of the word processor to order and re-order the instructions, or add missing ones. When the instructions have been completed, the children could print them out in a large font to be displayed alongside examples of surfaces joined using the methods they have described. They could also be given to other children. A class book of instructions could be put together for future reference.

Display ideas

Display various ways of joining a thin surface to another surface. Ask the children to make labels indicating what should and should not be done, and display these alongside the finished models.

FIXED UP   FPT

To develop knowledge and understanding of how well different glues and tapes join reclaimed materials. To use knowledge of how to use different-shaped materials for particular purposes. To work co-operatively.

†† *Large or small group.*

🕐 *Session 1: 45 minutes. Session 2: 30 minutes.*

⚠ *Make sure that the children know the rules for safe use of the glue gun.*

---

and bending up the strips, or cutting slots and flaps in each item and pushing them together. Try out the children's ideas, and add further suggestions if necessary. When there are several methods for the children to look at, talk with the children about making something using one of these ideas. Show them the items that you have prepared earlier and suggest that they make one of them, choosing their own decorative finish.

Suggestion(s) for extension

The children could make an item of their own choice incorporating the techniques. They could draw a design and write down instructions before they make their model.

Suggestion(s) for support

Break up the activity into several short activities, each focusing on a different way of joining a thin surface to another surface (such as flaps and slots). Children can be shown what to do, and then do it for themselves.

Assessment opportunities

Listen to the ideas that the children offer about joining something with a thin surface to another surface. Look at the finished product to see how well it is joined together.

Previous skills/knowledge needed

The children can use, build on and extend the knowledge about different ways of joining that they have gained from the 'Anyone can join' activity (page 34).

Key background information

There are several types of glue that could be used by the children.

▲ A glue gun can provide a strong join, and can be used to join plastic to another material; but there are dangers attached to using it. Certain LEAs ban the use of the glue gun by children, while others recommend that it is used only by teachers. Low temperature melt glue guns are recommended by many. Check what regulations apply.

▲ Masking tape can be used, removed and reused. Adhesive tape such as Sellotape provides a strong join, but it can easily get 'stuck up' and become unusable. If adhesive tape is removed, it tears paper and card and cannot be used again.

▲ A solid glue stick joins paper or thin card without mess, but is not always strong enough for thicker card or plastic.

▲ PVA glue can be used with paper, card, wood and some plastics, but it is crucial that the children use very small amounts.

Language to be introduced

join, glue, PVA glue, solid glue stick, sticky tape, masking tape, glue gun, spreader, movement, permanent

Preparation

Collect the glues, tapes and other materials and equipment which are to be used. Provide a collection of reclaimed materials, including items of different shapes and items made from different materials. Decide whether the children should make a model person or an animal. Prepare a chart (see Figure 5).

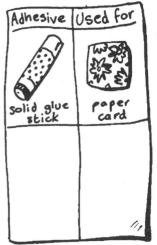

Adhesive	Used for
solid glue stick	paper card

Figure 5

Resources needed

PVA glue, glue spreaders, masking tape, adhesive tape, glue gun, glue stick, solid glue stick, a collection of reclaimed materials, a chart, paper and pencils.

What to do

Session 1

Tell the children that they are going to make a model person or animal. Talk with them about the different glues and tapes that they know, and how they have used these in the past. Show the children the collection of fixing materials. Look at each one and discuss its name, how it is used and what materials the children think that it might join together. Pay particular attention to the glue gun. Show them how it is used and who should use it (see note above). Make an entry in the chart for each item.

Make sure that the children understand that this investigation is about making a join that is permanent, and that the materials should be fixed together so that there is no relative movement (the model has no moving parts). Talk with the children about the different shapes that they will need for the head, body and arms and/or for the whole person or animal that they are going to make. Try out some different ideas that the children suggest, and ask them which glue or tape they would use.

While the children are constructing their model, encourage them to ask each other for help with holding pieces together. Throughout the activity, stress that it does not matter if they choose a glue or tape that does not work, as they can change it later. They are investigating what does and does not work best. Encourage them to produce something which has a quality finish.

When they have finished their model, ask them to draw their model on a sheet of paper and label it to show clearly which adhesives they have used for the different joins.

DESIGN AND TECHNOLOGY

Session 2

This can be done when the glues have dried. Ask the children to examine their models to determine which glues and tapes have worked well. Make additions to the chart to show which have worked well and which have not, and allow the children time to repair any joins that have come apart.

Suggestion(s) for extension

Ask the children to make their own model, using appropriate glues or tapes of something which they think their person or animal would like and use, such as a vehicle or a home.

Suggestion(s) for support

Some children may need help with using the glues or tapes. The range of options offered to some children could be restricted by using a smaller number of types of glue or tape.

Assessment opportunities

From the choices that the children make, it will be possible to assess their knowledge and understanding of how to use appropriate glues and tapes to join a range of materials. From watching them, it will be possible to see which children are able to work together and co-operate.

Opportunities for IT

The children could use the computer to create a simple database, either about the different types of sticky material they have used or about what method is best to stick different materials. The database could include the following fields:

Sticking material	masking tape
Used for	paper, card, plastic, wood
Not used for	fabrics
Good points	easily removed
Bad points	not good for small objects

An alternative would be to take different materials and see what means are appropriate for sticking them together:

Material	wood
Sellotape	no
Masking tape	no
Glue gun	yes
PVA adhesive	yes
Blu-Tack	no
Pritt Stick	no

This database could be extended as children try different materials and use different ways of sticking. It is a good idea to add some extra fields which can be left blank to start with, so that new methods can be added later on. The children could then use the database to search for the best way to stick different materials or identify the most versatile method of sticking.

Display ideas

Display the finished (decorated) models, and add labels to show how the joins were made, which joins worked well and which did not. Display large drawings of the different types of glues and tapes and add labels to show what they can join together. The reclaimed materials could be displayed instead of labels.

Textiles

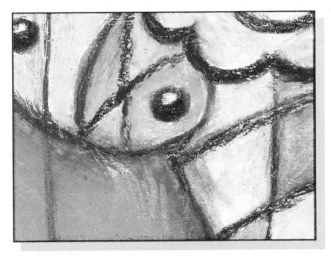

This section of the book contains IDEAs and FPTs relating to the use of textiles as construction materials. These activities will give children the opportunity to design and make with textiles, and to acquire knowledge and understanding relating to products and their purpose, people's needs and preferences, health and safety issues and appropriate vocabulary. The designing skills developed through these activities include discussion, modelling and evaluation of ideas, exploration and investigation of textiles, decoration and use of colour, shape and texture. The making skills developed include measuring, cutting, joining, using appropriate equipment, changing appearance and adding decoration. Knowledge and understanding are developed through experiences relating to the structure of textiles and how they are made, investigation and disassembly of textiles, evaluation of textile products (taking into account others' preferences, the quality of a product, how well it is made and how well it fits the purpose), the need for safe handling of tools and equipment and the importance of using the correct vocabulary.

The children can start by exploring textiles which are familiar to them and used in their everyday clothes. Other textiles, including those used in a range of cultures and in times past, can be introduced to the children. Appropriate contexts for work with textiles could include: celebrations, clothes, shops, festivals, puppets, toys, containers, the café.

⚠ It is important that all children are aware of the ways in which needles, pins and scissors should be handled. Make sure that the children wear aprons and do not touch any dyes with their hands.

GET IT TOGETHER! ◆ FPT

To develop children's familiarity with different fastenings and their uses.

†† *Whole-class discussion, then working in groups.*

🕐 *45 minutes.*

Previous skills/knowledge needed

The children can be encouraged to see links with ways of joining other materials, such as stapling and gluing paper and card. This activity can be linked to the FPT 'Anyone can join' (page 34), which relates to joining fabrics in different ways.

Key background information

There are many ways of joining fabrics, and different methods are used for different purposes. For example, a zip or Velcro may be used for something that needs to be opened and closed; stitches may be used to join fabric permanently in clothing or a container; glue may be used to add fabric decoration to a non-fabric product.

Language to be introduced

fastening, button, ribbon, zip, ace, glue, safety pin, join, press stud, hook and eye, toggle, stitch, elastic

Preparation

Make the collection of fastenings as outlined below, one for each group. Make a large chart on which to record the children's findings (see Figure 1). Have some good-quality paper ready for the drawings.

Fastenings	Used for?
⛓ zip	trousers
	jacket
〰 lace	shoe

Figure 1

Resources needed

A collection of fastenings, including a press stud and a hook and eye (ideally either sewn onto a piece of fabric or cut from an old garment), Velcro, a ribbon, a lace, a zip, a toggle, a button, elastic, a safety pin; Blu-Tack or masking tape; one copy per child of photocopiable sheet 131.

What to do

Ask the children to look at the clothes they are wearing, including their shoes. How are they fastened or joined together? Put up the information on the large chart that has been prepared. Draw the items and/or write their names. Can the children name any other fastenings?

Put out the collection of fastenings. Ask individual children to take one, name it and fix it with Blu-Tack or masking tape in the right place on the chart. If there are gaps, other items can be added later. Take one fastening and explore it with the children. What material is it made from? How does it work? When would you use it? Why?

Explain that the children will have time to explore the fastenings themselves and then to draw the fastening that they find most interesting. Put a collection on each table, and allow the children time to explore the fastenings. Encourage them to talk to each other about their discoveries. (They could work in pairs within their group.) Ask questions which will encourage the children to observe closely.

At the end of the activity, gather the children together and ask them for their ideas to fill in the 'Used for?' column on the chart. Finally, ask the children to fill in photocopiable sheet 131 as a way of reinforcing the activity.

Suggestions for extension

The children can continue to gather different textile fastenings (for example, from home). They could add to the class chart or record their findings by drawing and writing in a class book on fastenings. Clothing catalogues and magazine pictures could be used to provide photographs of unusual fastenings.

Suggestion(s) for support

The children can work on this activity a group at a time, to allow an adult to give more input. Groupings can be arranged such that some children can act as support for others.

Assessment opportunities

Photocopiable sheet 131 and the children's drawings will provide evidence of how well the children understand the purpose of fastenings and how they work. Note the children's comments when they are exploring the fastenings.

Opportunities for IT

Children could collect data about the different sorts of fastenings used on their clothes and display it using graphing software. The database used in the activity 'Fixed up' (page 46) could be extended to include fastenings for materials, or a new database could be set up for this purpose.

Display ideas

Make a large outline of a costumed person, such as a clown. Put on different fastenings to show different purposes: laces on shoes, buckle to hold up trousers, zip on trousers, button on waistcoat and so on.

Make a display of fastenings, together with the chart and the children's drawings from the activity.

Reference to photocopiable sheet

The children can complete photocopiable sheet 131 at the end of the activity. It can be used to assess their knowledge and understanding. They should draw in the blank circles appropriate fastenings for each of the objects. The teacher should decide whether their choice is appropriate: there may be more than one possible correct answer.

 BAGS, BAGS, BAGS ◀IDEA▶

To develop the children's understanding that the shape, size and material of a bag depends on its purpose.

†† *Class discussion, but individual recording sheet.*

🕐 *Session 1: 15 minutes; Session 2: 30–45 minutes; Session 3: 15 minutes.*

Previous skills/knowledge needed

It is useful, but not essential, for the children to have explored a collection of bags.

Key background information

In all cultures, bags are used to hold and carry things. They are made from different materials and have different shapes, sizes and colours because of their different uses.

Language to be introduced

bag, fabric, handle, strap, strong, material, fastening, join, pocket, waterproof

Preparation

Make a collection of fabric bags (such as a rucksack, evening bag, shopping bag, shoe bag and duffel bag) which are made from different materials, with different fastenings, and are used for a range of purposes.

Resources needed

A collection of bags (see above); quality drawing paper and materials.

What to do

This activity can be carried out in two or three separate sessions.

Session 1

Ask the children what they already know about bags. What is a bag? What do we use bags for? What can they be made from? How do they fasten or close up? Ask the children to record their ideas by drawing and writing on one half of a sheet of paper.

Session 2

Examine the collection of bags. Put them out so that the children can see them all; then look closely at them, one at a time. From the information which you have already gathered, it will be apparent how much the children already know and which areas need further exploration during your questioning.

▲ What is the bag used for?

▲ Who would use it?

▲ Think about the shape and size. Why has it been designed in that way? Is it easy to carry, attractive to look at, a similar shape to the items that go in it?

▲ What materials is the bag made from? Why have these been used?

▲ How are the sides joined together? Turn the bag inside out if possible, or look closely inside. What can the children tell you about the inside? (Seams, gussets, frayed edges.)

▲ How is the bag carried? (Straps, handles.)

▲ How are the handles fixed to the bag? (Sewn, staples, integral part of the bag.)

▲ Are parts of the bag strengthened? If so, how is this done? (Extra stitching, larger piece of material, double thickness, different material.)

▲ Are there any fastenings on the bag? What are they called? How do they work? Why have they, and not others, been used?

Now ask the children to choose a bag, draw it and label the drawing to record information about the bag.

Session 3

Ask the children to draw what they now know about bags on the other half of the paper used at the beginning of the activity. Encourage them to put in as much detail as possible. They may add labels or make exploded drawings of particular parts of the bag to show particular details. They could write down, or discuss with a friend, the new knowledge/ideas that they have gained.

Suggestion(s) for extension

Ask the children to evaluate baglike items made from textiles, such as hats, purses, comb cases and pencil cases, in a similar way.

The children could evaluate the bags in terms of attractiveness and explain why they prefer the appearance/ feel of a particular bag.

Look at bags from a range of cultures. (Use pictures if you do not have real artefacts.) In what ways are they similar? How do they differ? For example, in Japan people use a piece of fabric to tie around something and carry it by the knot.

Ask the children to research bags in times past. They could ask parents or grandparents what kinds of bags they

had. They could use books or link this with a visit to a museum, and record their information through drawings. Can they explain why bags have changed: technology, fashion, availability of resources?

Suggestion(s) for support

An adult or peer may need to write the labels for the drawings. Individual children may need to be encouraged to join in the discussion, with specific questions being directed at them.

Assessment opportunities

Use the drawings completed at the beginning and end of the activity to assess what ideas the children have. Look at the development from their initial drawing of a bag and their ideas at the end of the activity. Note particular relevant or irrelevant comments that children make during the discussion about bags.

Opportunities for IT

The children could use an art or drawing package to design their own bag, with a suitable motif. The designs could be printed out and displayed in the classroom.

The children could use a word processor to make labels for a classroom display of bags. Each label could give information about the material the bag is made from, what the bag might be used for and the advantages and disadvantages of the bag.

The children could use a simple database to store information about the bags that they bring to school. The fieldnames might include:

name	Balpinder
sex	boy
age	7
bag	yes
material	canvas
carrying	shoulder
fastening	zip
motif	Fabgear

The children could sort the database to see which materials or fastenings were the most common, or see how many children had a particular type of bag, or whether boys and girls had different preferences. The same headings could be used to collect data from different classes in the school.

Display ideas

Display a collection of bags together with an information sheet about each one.

Create an interactive display. Using catalogues, cut out pictures of different bags and a variety of items that might be appropriate to put in them. Attach pictures of different bags to the wall, and put the pictures of various items with some Blu-Tack in a box underneath the display. The children can then stick items next to the appropriate bag, using Blu-Tack.

SORTING FABRICS ◇IDEA

To develop the children's knowledge and understanding of how different fabrics are made in different ways, have different properties and are suitable for different purposes.

†† *Class or group activity.*

🕐 *30 minutes.*

Previous skills/knowledge needed

The children should be able to use a magnifying glass. It would be useful to remind the children of how they have carried out other observation activities.

Key background information

Through careful observation of a variety of fabrics, it will be important to bring out in discussion that there are many different fabrics which have different appearances and properties and are suitable for different purposes. The children should experience fabrics which are, for example, waterproof, used for decoration, hard-wearing, used to help us keep warm or cool.

Language to be introduced

appearance, fabric, fluffy, soft, porous (with holes), thin, smooth, crease, stretchy, furry, thick, rough, transparent (see-through), waterproof, opaque (not see-through)

Preparation

Decide whether this will be a whole-class or a group activity. Ensure that the collection of fabrics includes both natural and synthetic fabrics, and fabrics with a range of properties, such as: velvet, net, lace, satin, knitted fabric, woven fabric, corduroy, felt, hessian, polyester. Prepare a large chart on which to record findings. Make enlarged (A3 size) copies of photocopiable sheet 128 (see activity on page 38).

Resources needed

A collection of five or six different fabrics, one for each group; magnifying glasses, one between two children; a chart; two small hoops for each group; scissors that will cut the fabric; fabric glue or Copydex and spreaders; one enlarged (A3) copy per child of photocopiable sheet 128.

What to do

Display a selection of fabrics so that all the children can see them. Explain that they will have some time to explore these fabrics for themselves. Ask them what kind of observations they might make. They may suggest seeing whether the fabrics crease easily, tear, crumple, are stiff, are heavy, are thick and so on. Now let the children explore the fabrics on their own. Encourage them to observe closely and talk to each other about their findings. They could use a magnifying glass, smell the fabrics, scrunch them up, pull them, feel them with their fingertips, rub them gently on their cheeks.

Now collect observations from all the children. To focus their investigation, ask them to sort the fabrics. Ask the children for their own criteria for sorting; then suggest further criteria, one at a time. Ask the children to work as a group and sort the fabrics into two hoops. Does everyone agree? Criteria to try might include thick/thin, soft/rough, transparent/opaque, creases easily/does not crease easily, smells/does not smell, pretty/not pretty, stretchy/not stretchy, fluffy/not fluffy, furry/not furry, and porous/waterproof. Put the sets into hoops. To record the activity individually, the children can choose a criterion and then sort, cut and stick pieces of the fabric into the correct sets, using photocopiable sheet 128.

Suggestion(s) for extension

Extend the range of fabrics to be investigated.

The children can be encouraged to think about overlapping sets. Prepare a sheet for the children with two overlapping circles, as an introduction to Venn diagrams.

The children can carry out a range of scientific investigations to find out the properties of a fabric such as its absorbency, waterproofness or tearability. They could choose three or four different fabrics and, for example, test whether they are waterproof by pouring the same amount of water onto each one in turn and observing what happens.

DESIGN AND TECHNOLOGY

Suggestion(s) for support

Use fewer fabrics for the children to investigate. The vocabulary can be modified – for example, saying *see-through* for *transparent*. Children may need help to cut the fabric.

Assessment opportunities

Note the comments that the children make when they are involved in their own investigation of the fabrics. Check the children's recording to see whether they can make sets that fit a criterion.

Opportunities for IT

The children could create a database on the fabrics they investigate, recording the data from each of the criteria that they have used for sorting. The fieldnames might include:

fabric	wool
thick/thin	thick
soft/rough	soft
creases	no
smell	yes

The data could either be added by answering *yes/no* or by using appropriate words, as in the example above. The children could use the database to answer such questions as:

▲ Which fabrics are soft?
▲ Which fabrics do not crease easily?
▲ Which fabrics are rough and have a smell?

Display ideas

Display a large chart with fabric samples stuck on and the words that the children have used to describe each fabric written alongside (see Figure 2).

Figure 2

Alongside different pieces of fabric, encourage the children to attach (with Blu-Tack or masking tape) pictures of items of clothing (cut from magazines and catalogues) which could be made from the fabric. This could be carried out over a period of time. Check each day to see whether the children are choosing appropriate pictures.

Reference to photocopiable sheet

The children select a criterion and then sort, cut and stick pieces of fabric in the appropriate circles on photocopiable sheet 128.

THE RIGHT HAT   IDEA

To develop the children's skill in evaluating a ready-made product.

✝✝ *Large group.*
🕐 *30 minutes.*

Previous skills/knowledge needed

Links can be made with other evaluation work that the children have undertaken.

Key background information

Through discussion of the collection of hats, the children should develop their understanding that products are made for a purpose and that people have different likes and dislikes.

Language to be introduced

hat, like, preference, dislike, brim, felt, straw, plastic, hatband, cap, helmet, bonnet, beret, sun hat, rain hat

Preparation

A few days before the activity, display some hats. These could include hats for swimming, the sun, weddings, winter, skiing and cycling. Encourage the children to talk about them by placing some open-ended questions around the display, such as:

▲ What are the hats needed for?
▲ When would you wear the hats?
▲ Why is this hat made from hard plastic?

Resources needed

A collection of real hats, made from different fabrics and used for various purposes (examples might include sun hats, wedding hats, party hats, rain hats and baby hats); a variety of drawing materials.

What to do

Put out the hats so that the children can see them. Start with a general discussion about the hats, drawing on the children's ideas. Which colours do they like/dislike? Which shape do they like the best? Ask them to explain their decisions.

Then take each hat in turn. What purpose do they think the hat is meant for? What makes them think that? Help them to identify the criteria for making the hat suit its purpose. (For example, a sunhat needs a wide brim.) Think about the material it is made from, its shape, its size, its colour, its fastenings. Does the hat feel comfortable to wear? What changes would they make to improve it?

Ask the children to choose the hat that they like best and then draw it carefully. They should include as much detail as possible, and add labels to the drawing to show the reasons for their choice of hat. When they have finished, display the drawings and compare the choices that the children made. Did they all prefer the same hat? If not, what were the reasons for the differences?

Suggestion(s) for extension

The children could design a hat for a specific purpose and show through their drawing and labels that it is effective for this purpose.

Suggestion(s) for support

Help the children to add labels to their drawing to show their reasons for choosing the hat. Some children may need further discussion to help them understand that factors such as material and shape are partly determined by the specific purpose of the hat.

Assessment opportunities

Listen to the children's comments and look at their drawings to assess which children can make sensible judgements about the collection of hats.

Opportunities for IT

The children could use a simple art of drawing package to design a hat for a particular purpose, such as keeping the sun off or keeping your ears warm in the winter.

Display ideas

Make a display of the hats, using papier-mâché heads and a painted or collage background to show the context in which each hat would be worn. Display the drawings or computer pictures that the children have made alongside this.

FABRIC FASTENERS ◈ FPT

To develop the children's practical skill in making different joins with fabrics.

†† *A group working as individuals.*

⏲ *Session 1: 30–45 minutes (can be repeated). Session 2: 20–30 minutes.*

⚠ *The children must be fully aware of the dangers of needles, scissors and staples.*

Previous skills/knowledge needed

The children should be able to thread a needle and to sew back stitch and running stitch. They should have evaluated a range of bought fastenings and understand how these work, as in the activity 'Get it together!' (page 50). The children should appreciate how different fastenings are used for different purposes.

Key background information

The children will have the opportunity to make some decisions for themselves within a limited range of options. They will join pieces of fabric using various methods. It is important to stress that the children should use only a very small quantity of glue.

Language to be introduced

fastening, button, ribbon, zip, lace, glue, safety pin, join, press stud, hook and eye, toggle, stitch, back stitch, running stitch, elastic

Preparation

Cut up fabric to make a large number of small squares or rectangles (6–7cm side). Make sure that there is sufficient equipment for each child in the group. Make enlarged (A3) copies of photocopiable sheet 132. The activity 'Get it together!' (page 50) is a suitable preparation for this activity.

Resources needed

Fabric for cutting up, plastic needles, threads, scissors, a stapler and staples, safety pins, glue, laces, ribbon, Velcro, press studs, hooks and eyes, A3 sheets of card, one enlarged (A3) copy per child of photocopiable sheet 132.

What to do

This task can be carried out in two sessions at different times.

Session 1

Remind the children about the different fastenings they have explored, and put them out on the table. Explain that they are going to learn how to join fabrics in different ways and then, through a display, show others these ways. They have to try the joins shown on the photocopiable sheet first, and then they can make any other joins they think of. Check that the children know how to use each method by asking

DESIGN AND TECHNOLOGY

individual children to demonstrate how to (for example) staple, sew or glue two pieces of fabric together. Let the children work on their own as much as possible, using each other for support.

Session 2

When the children have finished making their joins, discuss with them what they might use the different joins for. For example: running stitch for making a soft toy, so the stuffing does not fall out of gaps; staples for a quick join on a finger puppet (the staples could be covered by gluing fabric on top); Velcro for a fastening on a bag, so it can be opened and closed. Then give each child a large sheet of card and ask them to stick their filled-in copy of photocopiable sheet 132 onto it and decorate the border. The sheets can then be used for display.

Suggestion(s) for extension

The children can add different joins to new copies of the photocopiable sheet and display them.

Suggestion(s) for support

Work with individual children and ask them to use each fastening in turn.

Assessment opportunities

Note the children who cannot work without the support of others and cannot extract relevant information from the activity sheet. Check the end products for those children who are able to join the fabrics in various ways.

Opportunities for IT

The children could use a word processor or desktop publishing package to create labels for the fastenings they are displaying, indicating when they would use each fastening and its advantages and disadvantages. They could use different fonts, styles and sizes, so that the display will be easy to read from a distance.

Display ideas

Display the finished mounted sheets together with a collection of fastenings which the children can touch and use. Display a collection of items which have the same type of fastening (such as buttons), to show how it can be used on different items.

Reference to photocopiable sheet

Photocopiable sheet 132 is an activity sheet which helps the children to follow diagrams and to join their fabrics in different ways. They will make the different joins shown on the sheet, then create two of their own and draw them in the two empty boxes.

USING A PATTERN

To develop the children's knowledge and understanding of a pattern and how to use it. To develop and extend their ability to cut out accurately.

†† *Class discussion, then groups for the practical work.*

🕐 *Discussion 15–20 minutes. Practical work 20–30 minutes.*

⚠ *Make sure that the children handle the pins correctly and put them into a container with a lid. Use plastic-headed pins.*

Previous skills/knowledge needed

This activity builds on the children's ability to cut paper and fabric accurately.

Key background information

A pattern can be used to ensure that something is cut out to the right shape and size – and thus to produce a large number of goods that are exactly the same. The pattern can be made from thin paper and pinned onto fabric. The children may be familiar with drawing around templates; this is a similar idea.

Language to be introduced

pattern, shape, pin, size

Preparation

Check that you have a pattern and a finished item to match, such as a soft toy. (You may need to buy these.) Make enlarged (A3) copies of photocopiable sheet 133; cut out two or three of the shapes from a copy, for your own use.

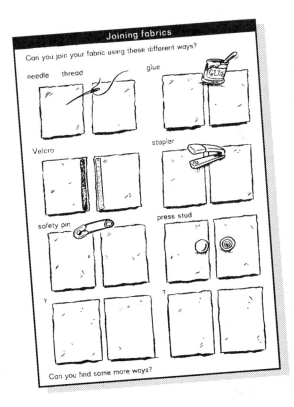

On large sheets of card, prepare backgrounds for the winter and summer seasons (see illustration).

winter

Resources needed

A pattern and matching item, a variety of fabrics, fabric or Copydex glue with spreaders, scissors that will cut fabric, seasonal backgrounds on which to put cut-out images, one A3 copy per child of photocopiable sheet 133, two or three patterns cut out from this sheet.

What to do

First discuss with the children the meaning of the word 'pattern'. They may be used to creating repetitive patterns with shapes and colours. When we make clothes, we use a pattern [like a template] to make sure we have the right size and shape pieces of fabric for our garments.

Now show the children a pattern and ask them to look carefully at it. Can they guess what it will be used to make? Have the ready-made item to show them. Why is the paper for the pattern so thin?

Take the small patterns that you have cut out from the A3 copy of photocopiable sheet 133. Explain that you are going to put them on some fabric, ready to cut out the shapes. Where should you put them? Encourage the children to think about the importance of not wasting fabric. Ask them how you will attach the patterns to the fabric so that you can take them off again. Have some large pins ready, and let one or two children help with the task. Ask them to think about where they will place the pins. If they are too near the edge of the pattern, it will be impossible to cut the fabric; if they are in the middle, the fabric will move about. Make sure that the fabric and the pattern are flat. Cut out the shape and remove the pins and pattern. Show the children the pattern and the cut-out piece of fabric, so that they can see that they are the same size and shape.

Explain to the children that they are going to make, from fabric, a picture of clothes for different seasons. Ask them to choose one pattern and to think carefully about the fabric that they will use. Should a swimming costume be made from thick woolly material? Should a winter coat be made from thin, porous material? The children can place and pin their pattern on the fabric, cut it out and use fabric glue to stick it on the background. Remind them to use a very small quantity of glue.

Suggestion(s) for extension

The children could create their own patterns and individual pictures. Possible themes include minibeasts and trees. They could sew their items of clothing onto a cut-out person.

Suggestion(s) for support

The children may need help from an adult or peer to pin and cut around the pattern.

Assessment opportunities

Look to see whether the children have wasted fabric, have pinned their pattern on correctly and have cut out neatly.

Opportunities for IT

The children could use a simple drawing program to create their own patterns. If the background grid is turned on, it will help children to create symmetrical patterns (for example, a glove puppet) so that the two sides match. These could be printed, cut out and used. The children may need to use the software's enlargement facility to make their original design fit an A4 sheet of paper. Alternatively, you could use the enlargement facility on a photocopier if the original is too small.

Display ideas

Display the finished pictures along with a step-by-step guide to making them by using a pattern.

The children could use a pattern and cut out shapes from felt to decorate a Christmas tree, a frieze or a place mat.

Reference to photocopiable sheet

The children only cut out one pattern from photocopiable sheet 133 to start with. The sheets can be placed on the group table, and the children can choose which shape they are going to make.

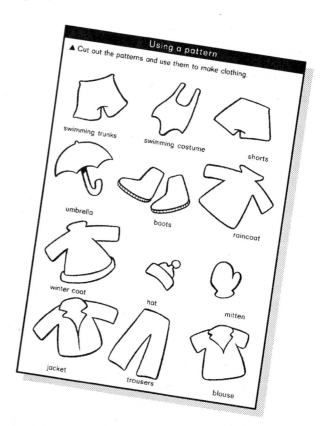

Using a pattern
▲ Cut out the patterns and use them to make clothing.

swimming trunks · swimming costume · shorts · umbrella · boots · raincoat · winter coat · hat · mitten · jacket · trousers · blouse

DESIGN AND TECHNOLOGY

A SPECIAL CASE ◆ FPT

To develop and extend the children's knowledge and understanding of patterns. To develop the children's ability to join fabrics and produce a quality finish.

†† *Group work.*

⏱ *Session 1: 30–40 minutes; Session 2: 30–40 minutes.*

⚠ *Make sure that the children handle the needles and pins correctly. The needles should be pushed into pads and stored in a lidded container.*

Previous skills/knowledge needed

The children should understand the purpose of the pattern; it would help if they have completed the activity 'Using a pattern' (page 56).

Key background information

A pattern can be used to ensure that something is the right shape and size. It can be used to produce a large number of goods that are identical. The pattern can be made from thin paper, to make it easy to pin onto fabric. A seam is put around the shape on the pattern to ensure that the size is correct when the case is turned inside-out. Stitches can be used to join two pieces of fabric; to achieve a quality finish, the stitches should be small and of the same size. This activity could be linked with the IDEA 'Sorting fabrics' (page 53).

Language to be introduced

sew, thread, pattern, pin, seam, needle, shape, size

Preparation

Make sure that you have a pattern with a matching item (you may need to buy these to add to your school resources) and some fabric. Make a case based on the design that the children will use. Decide whether the children should make the case out of one fabric (such as felt) or a variety of fabrics.

Resources needed

A pattern and matching item, one copy per child of photocopiable sheet 134, thin paper (such as kitchen paper) from which to make the pattern, scissors that will cut paper and fabric, large plastic needles (one for each child), a variety of coloured threads, fabric for the cases, plastic-headed pins.

What to do

This activity can be carried out in two sessions at different times, or all at one time.

Session 1

Discuss the children's ideas about patterns, drawing on the activity 'Using a pattern' (page 56). Remind them about the need for a pattern to keep the right shape and size for their product. Then show the children the case you have made. What do they think they will need to make one? How will they cut out the right shape? Now show them the pattern for the case. Ask one child to show everyone how it should be pinned on the fabric. It may be necessary to remind the children about the importance of not wasting fabric. Ask the children how many pieces they will need to cut to make one case. Let the children cut out the pattern from photocopiable sheet 134, pin it onto their fabric, cut out the case (make sure they cut out two pieces) and then take off the patterns. Make sure that the pins are put safely into a container.

Session 2

Show the children that the case can be sewn up the sides and then turned inside-out, thus hiding the stitching. Remind the children about the dotted line on the pattern (you could show the pattern again) and explain that when the children turn the case inside-out, the space inside the case will be smaller than before. Show them an item of clothing with a seam. Then show or remind the children how to start sewing by threading the needle and making two or three little stitches. The children can use running stitch or backstitch. Encourage them to keep their stitches small, neat and equal-sized. When they have finished, remind them to oversew two or three small stitches in order to finish off and to stop the thread from unravelling. Finally, they should put a comb or a few pencils into the case and evaluate the success of the design.

Suggestion(s) for extension

The children could create their own pattern. They could add decoration to the case – for example, using embroidery or sticking on fabric shapes.

Suggestion(s) for support

A child may need one-to-one help to pin, cut out and/or sew. A peer or an adult could provide this support. It may be necessary to have further discussion about the seam and why it is needed.

Assessment opportunities

Watch to see which children understand how a pattern should be used and what a seam is for.

Opportunities for IT

The children could use a simple drawing program to create their own pattern for the pencil case, or to design a decoration for the finished pattern. If the background grid is turned on and set at 1cm intervals, it will help the children to get the dimensions correct. The patterns can be printed, cut out and used.

Display ideas

Draw a flow diagram to show how a pattern is used to make the case. The children can fill this in with their illustrations and writing. Display the cases, together with questions relating to the idea of fitness for a purpose:

▲ Could you keep a comb or pencils in these?
▲ Will the pencils or comb fall out of the sides?
▲ Are the cases large enough?
▲ Are they attractive to look at?

Reference to photocopiable sheet

Photocopiable sheet 134 can be used as a pattern for designing. Make sure that the children cut out the pattern accurately.

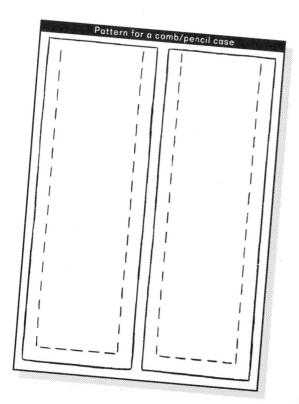
Pattern for a comb/pencil case

ABSOLUTELY FABRIC FPT

To develop the children's awareness of how decoration (such as printing and painting) can enhance the look of fabric. To develop the children's ability to decorate fabric.

†† *Whole-class discussion. Practical work in groups.*
🕐 *Session 1: 10–15 minutes for discussion, 20 minutes for practical work. Session 2: 10–15 minutes.*

Previous skills/knowledge needed

The children can draw on any previous experiences relating to the use of colour, printing and patterns.

Key background information

The appearance of fabric can be changed and improved in many ways. It is possible to print or draw on it, or add other decorations such as sequins.

Language to be introduced

appearance, print, pattern, fabric paint, raised paints, fabric pens, decoration, sequins, glitter

Preparation

Cover a table with paper and put out the equipment in the centre, so that it is within reach of each child working at the table. Decide what the design concept will be. Examples could include colours, shapes, letters or numbers. Cut up plain fabric for printing (approx. 15cm square pieces).

Resources needed

One piece of fabric for each child (see above), aprons, fabric paints, items to print with (such as cotton reels, plastic shapes and bottle tops), raised paints, fabric pens, sequins, fabric glue or Copydex and spreaders, newspaper, pieces of sponge, paint brushes, drawing materials.

What to do

Session 1

First discuss with the children the word *pattern* and its different meanings. We can make a 'pattern' to decorate something, but we can use a 'pattern' to make an item of clothing. Now show the children a collection of plain and printed fabrics. Ask which ones the children like and why they like them. Can the children think how the colour and pattern get onto the fabric? Using a simple block and fabric paints, explain about printing. Although you can change the appearance of only a small amount of fabric by hand, machines can print large quantities very fast.

Show the children the fabric paints and the items that they can use for printing, and explain that they are going to make a large wall display or hanging. Each of them will have a piece of fabric to print on and decorate. Show them how to spread the fabric paint on the surface that they will use

---

for printing, to place the surface carefully onto the fabric, to press and then to lift it off carefully. Let one or two children try so the others can see. Use old fabric for the demonstration, to show the children how important it is not to waste materials.

Before the children print their final design, they can practise on paper to choose their pattern and their colour. Get the children to draw their pattern (choosing from the shapes that are available) and to colour it in (choosing from the fabric paints). When they are satisfied with their design, they can put on an apron, write their name on the back of their piece of fabric and then print onto their fabric using fabric paints. The prints should be left to dry.

Session 2

Later, the children could stick on coloured sequins or use raised fabric paints to add to the printed pattern. Make sure that the children draw their design first, so that they know what colours and shapes they want to add. If the fabric pieces are being used to make a wall hanging (see 'Display ideas'), then an adult will need to sew them all together.

Suggestion(s) for extension

Children can make their own printing block from raised material (such as polystyrene shapes stuck onto a piece of card) and print onto another piece of their fabric. They could then use their pieces of fabric for a variety of projects: a quilt, a cushion cover, a table mat, curtains, a card, a book cover and so on.

Suggestion(s) for support

The children may need help to make sure that the object is covered evenly with paint. They may need help pressing their objects onto the fabric. Check that they are able to write their names on their pieces of fabric.

Assessment opportunities

Through discussion, evidence of the children's knowledge and understanding of printing and decorating fabric can be collected. During the practical work, it will be possible to assess the children's ability to create a design and to realise their design as a finished product.

Opportunities for IT

The children could use an art package to create their own pattern before printing it. If they are shown how to use the 'cut and paste' or 'copy facility, they can make multiple copies of their original printing design and then arrange them on the screen to make their pattern. They can experiment with full or half drop patterns, or even rotate their pattern to make a more interesting design. It is also possible to use special transfer paper which can be put into a colour printer to allow the designed pattern to be printed onto fabric.

Display ideas

The children's printed fabric pieces could be stitched together to form a wall hanging. The patterns that the children have printed could be reprinted with paint on paper, and displayed alongside patterns that they have made with a graphics program.

THE WORK OF THE WEAVERS FPT

To develop the children's knowledge and their understanding of how fabrics can be made by weaving. To develop their ability to weave.

†† *Group work.*

🕐 *60 minutes.*

Previous skills/knowledge needed

The children may draw on paper-weaving experiences (if they have these) and the IDEA 'Sorting fabrics' (page 53).

Key background information

The *warp* is the long downward strand in a woven fabric, and the *weft* is the strand that is woven in and out of the warp. Fabric is made by weaving the weft under and over the warp.

Language to be introduced

warp, weaving, scrim, weft, netting

DESIGN AND TECHNOLOGY

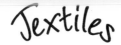

Preparation

Collect enough pieces of woven fabric to provide one for each pair of children. Cut up the netting or scrim (approx. 15cm square for each child). Make sure that there is a range of colours and textures in the yarns and fabrics. Cut the stiff card to size, a little smaller than the size of the piece of netting or scrim, two pieces for each child.

Resources needed

Landscape pictures, a collection of woven fabrics, magnifying glasses, scrim or netting (from vegetable bags), scissors that will cut fabric, stiff card, masking tape. A selection of yarns, ribbons and strips of fabrics.

What to do

Show the children pieces of woven material. Ask them to look at these closely through a magnifying glass and then gently to pull the threads apart. Can they see how the threads are woven together? Take a piece of netting or scrim and start to weave through some fabric or thick ribbon. Let one or two children try this.

Now show the children a picture of a landscape. What colours can they see? Think about the different 'layers' such as the sky, fields, buildings. Ask them to look at the things that they have for weaving (such as fabrics, ribbons, yarns) and ask a child to choose something suitable for the sky. Start to weave with it to show the children how to build up a layer.

Give the children their own piece of netting; let them choose their picture and weave their landscape. Encourage them to use a variety of things with which to weave, and to change colours to create the landscape scene. When it is finished, the children can mount the landscape on thick card, turn the edges under and stick them down with masking tape. To give the product a quality finish, another piece of card can be placed over the back to cover the edging. (The children should understand the reason for doing this.) The woven landscapes can be displayed to link with work in geography, or used as covers for books.

Suggestion(s) for extension

The children could weave a landscape of their own design, or weave a piece of cloth to make into a small comb case or purse.

Suggestion(s) for support

Some children may need help to weave their fabric strip or yarn into and out of the warp. Some children may need help to mount their weaving on card; they could work in pairs to do this.

Assessment opportunities

The finished product will show whether the child can weave correctly. Note how much support was given.

Opportunities for IT

The children could use an art package to design their own landscape picture, to be used as a basis for their weaving.

Display ideas

Display the finished products beside the original landscape pictures. Make a display of different woven fabrics, perhaps showing different kinds of weave (balanced weave, warp-face weave, weft-face weave, twill weave, double weave and so on).

The children could make a large drawing of how to weave, and surround it with observational drawings of woven fabric.

STITCHED UP   FPT

To develop the children's knowledge and understanding of different stitches and their uses.

†† *Small group, working as individuals.*

🕒 *30 minutes (activity can be repeated as new stitches are introduced).*

⚠ *Make sure that the needles are stored in a fabric pad inside a lidded container. Plastic needles are safer to use than steel ones.*

Previous skills/knowledge needed

The children can draw on any previous experience of sewing that they have.

Key background information

There are different stitches, made in different ways, for different purposes. If a thread is too long for sewing, it will become tangled.

DESIGN AND TECHNOLOGY

Language to be introduced

needle, thread, stitch, blanket stitch, back stitch, cross stitch, running stitch, chain stitch, Binka

Preparation

Make a collection of items with embroidery on them, such as a sampler. Provide a range of different-coloured threads and enough Binka, needles and scissors for the children to use. Make an example of each stitch to show the children, and cut the Binka into a suitable size for a bookmark.

Resources needed

A collection of embroidery work, plastic needles, coloured threads, scissors, Binka, one copy per child (or small group) of photocopiable sheet 135.

What to do

Start by showing the children some pieces of work which include different stitches for decoration, such as a sampler. Talk with them about sewing, and find out whether any of them know how to make particular stitches. Talk with them about the colours and patterns that have been used. Show them the piece of Binka that they are going to use and the choice of threads available. Talk about the thickness of the threads – threads used for embroidery are thicker than the thread used to sew clothes. Show them how to thread a needle, how to cut a thread (the length from the elbow to hand), how to start sewing by making two or three little stitches, and how to do a running stitch.

Now give the children the photocopiable sheet and explain that they can use this to see how the finished product might look and to remind themselves about different stitches. Let the children start sewing, using running stitch. When the first children finish, stop the group and show them a cross stitch. Continue as before, introducing blanket stitch and chain stitch as appropriate. Encourage the children to think about their choice of colours and the neatness of the stitches. When the sewing is finished, encourage them to evaluate their own and others' work. Which patterns do they think look good and why? Which colours do they think look good together? Which do not?

Suggestion(s) for extension

Ask the children to draw a design for stitching on a piece of paper, deciding which colours to use and whether the pattern will go up and down or round and round. Then they can make the pattern on a bookmark.

Suggestion(s) for support

Individual children may need help (from adults or peers) to form the stitches. Introduce one new stitch at each activity time.

Assessment opportunities

The finished bookmark will be evidence of the children's ability to embroider using different stitches. Note which children needed much or only a little support.

Opportunities for IT

The children could use an art or drawing package to draw out their design before they start. If a background grid is set up the teacher to start with and saved onto disk, the children can load in this file and then decide which squares and colours will be used to make their sampler. Some software, such as 'Tiler' (for the ACORN series of computers), automatically creates symmetrical patterns as children colour in specific tiles on their starting grid.

Display ideas

Display the finished products together with large drawings of the different stitches and how to make them. The bookmarks could be kept in the book corner and attached to the wall in transparent holders, so that they can be removed for use and then replaced.

Reference to photocopiable sheet

Photocopiable sheet 135 is used for reference purposes, to show the children how their finished bookmark might look and how to make different stitches. The children can then keep the sheet for future work involving stitching.

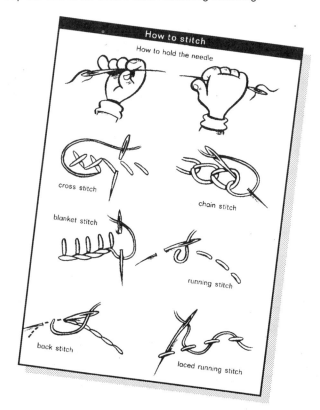

DESIGN AND TECHNOLOGY

Food

This chapter contains IDEAs and FPTs relating to the use of food in construction. Through these activities, children will have the opportunity to design and make food products and to acquire knowledge and understanding of various food products and their functions, people's needs and preferences, safety, health and hygiene and appropriate vocabulary. The designing skills developed include discussion and modelling of ideas, decorating and the use of colour, shape and texture. The making skills developed include measuring, combining, spreading, stirring, mixing, cutting, grating and the use of appropriate equipment.

The children's knowledge and understanding develop through investigations into different foods and their appearance and taste and the evaluation of food products, taking into account others' preferences. The children will develop an understanding that a healthy diet is necessary; that foods can be grouped in different ways; that factors such as individual, family and cultural preferences help determine the kinds of food we eat; and that safety and hygiene are important when working with food.

Children should understand that food must not be wasted. Thus some of their work relating to development of skills such as cutting, shaping, combining and designing can involve food substitutes such as salt dough, before they use actual foods for design and make assignments.

The following contexts are appropriate for work with food: celebrations, festivals, our home, shops, journeys, out and about and our local environment or community.

⚠ Before food is handled or tasted, any food allergies or dietary restrictions must be checked with the children's parents or guardians.

DO IT CLEAN   FPT

To develop knowledge and understanding of safe and hygienic working.

†† *Class or group work; individual recording.*

🕐 *30 minutes.*

Previous skills/knowledge needed

It would be helpful to link this activity with other areas of the curriculum, such as PE, where these considerations are important.

Key background information

It is important to work safely and hygienically with food. To get rid of bacteria, all pieces of equipment should be clean and not handled before use. After use, they need to be washed in hot, soapy water to remove food and bacteria, then dried and stored in clean, airtight containers to keep them clean for the next time they are needed. The area in which food will be used should be prepared carefully. Surfaces should be wiped down with disinfectant spray and covered with plastic, washable cloths. The children need to prepare themselves for working with food by tying back their hair, taking off rings, putting on a clean apron and washing their hands. Fingers must not be put into food to taste the mixture. Utensils and other equipment must be used correctly to make sure that no-one causes an accident.

Language to be introduced

safety, health, hygiene, disinfect, allergic, clean, disinfectant, spray, plastic apron, utensils, fork, spoon, bowl, knife, sieve, washing-up liquid, tea towel, oven

Working with food

hair tied back

sleeves back

no rings

clean hands

apron on

Preparation

Collect the equipment listed below.

Resources needed

A table, a plastic cloth, a disinfectant spray, two clean cloths, four plastic aprons, a fork, a spoon, a knife, a bowl, a sieve, a small quantity of flour or sugar, washing-up facilities (including washing-up liquid, tea towel) oven, one copy per child of photocopiable sheet 136, writing materials.

What to do

Start by asking the children about the preparations they have to make in order to take part in different activities at school. What do they have to do for PE, for play time, for dinner time and for art work? Why do they need to do these things? They should begin to think about ideas relating to safety and hygiene for these familiar activities.

Then gather the children round a table which you have set up ready for work with food. First, ask them about the utensils. How should each piece be used? Why is it important that they be used properly? What will happen to the utensils when they have been used? Why do we use hot water and washing up-liquid when we wash the equipment? Why do we dry it and put it away in a covered place? Why do we need a clean tea towel frequently?

DESIGN AND TECHNOLOGY

Now look at the table. Why is it covered in a plastic cloth? Scatter something on the cloth, such as sugar or flour. How can we clean the table? Have a wash cloth and some disinfectant to hand. Show the children the oven (if appropriate). Talk with them about how hot the oven is, and the importance of not touching it and always listening to instructions from an adult when their group is using the oven.

Bring out two children (both with long hair) and prepare one only for working with food. Ask the rest of the class what differences they can see now between the two children. Why do they think you have done this? Now give the children the copies of photocopiable sheet 136. Ask them to make the outlined person into a boy or a girl and to draw her/him so that he/she is ready to work safely and hygienically with food.

Suggestion(s) for extension
The children could make a poster to show an area for food work that is prepared correctly and one that is not.

Suggestion(s) for support
Some children may need to work in a small group for this activity, to make sure that they understand how to act safely. You could ask individual children questions about particular aspects to check that they have understood.

Assessment opportunities
Through their work on photocopiable sheet 136, the children will show their ideas about working with food hygienically and safely.

Opportunities for IT
Children could work in pairs, using a word processor or desktop publishing package to write and print a list of instructions for working safely and hygenically with food. The keyboarding time could be reduced if each pair adds one instruction to the class list. The list could then be printed in a large font, to be displayed in the classroom.

Display ideas
Display the completed photocopiable sheets which the children have made as their recording of the activity. As a contrast, the children could fill in sheets showing what *not* to do.

Cut out a life-sized outline of a child and help the children to dress and prepare the child outline ready for working with food. They could use paint or coloured crayons, or use fabrics to make a collage.

Reference to photocopiable sheet
The children can choose whether to make the outline on photocopiable sheet 136 into a boy or a girl. They should add clothes appropriately, then choose the correct label from the box to go at the end of each line.

TASTES AND TEXTURES
IDEA

To develop awareness that foods have different tastes and textures. To develop appropriate vocabulary to describe different textures and tastes.

†† *Small-group activity, individual photocopiable sheets.*

⏰ *30 minutes.*

⚠ *Be aware of any food allergies or dietary restrictions that may affect this activity.*

Previous skills/knowledge needed
Through discussion before the activity, the children can be encouraged to think about familiar tastes and textures of food.

Key background information
Foods have different tastes and textures, and during the activity the children should be encouraged to develop and use specific vocabulary that is used to describe these. They should also understand that not all people like the same tastes and textures, and that nothing is wrong with this.

Language to be introduced
taste, texture, bitter, sweet, sour, tangy, tasteless, creamy, spicy, salty, chewy, crunchy, juicy, smooth, sticky

Preparation
Prepare a picture of an open mouth on which to record the

Tastes and textures

Tastes

Food	Tastes like...	I like it	It's OK	I do not like it

Textures

Food	Feels like...	I like it	It's OK	I do not like it

Let a number of different children try the same food. Ask them for words that describe what they taste and feel, and put these up on a chart beside the name and/or picture of the food that they are tasting. Take some time over this. Encourage the children to eat slowly and to let their tongues move over the food.

Now explain that they are each going to taste all the foods, one at a time. Which tastes and textures do the children like and dislike? Can they give reasons for this? Ask the children for words to describe the tastes and textures. Help them to fill in a row on the photocopiable sheet after each tasting.

Suggestion(s) for extension

Let the children investigate (by tasting various food products) how different cooking or preserving methods affect the taste and texture of a given food. For example, how do they prefer potatoes to be cooked? Why? Ask the children to predict tastes and textures before they carry out the testing.

Suggestion(s) for support

An adult can work with an individual child to develop his or her use of specific vocabulary. Peer or adult support can be given to enable the child to complete the activity sheet. Pictures rather than words could be used on the activity sheet.

Assessment opportunities

Evidence of the children's understanding that different foods have different tastes and textures can be gathered from the activity sheet, and from the words that individual children use when describing the tastes and textures verbally.

children's words. Set out the various foods on another table, then cover them up in case the children are distracted by them. Have a list of key words which you want the children to use. Make an enlarged (A3) copy of photocopiable sheet 137 for your own use.

Resources needed

A collection of foods that have different tastes and textures, such as crisps, crackers, ready-made custard, a banana, a lemon, an orange, a cake, fudge, chocolate, a spicy paste or dip, curry sauce; plastic cutlery; paper towels; small plastic containers for each type of food; washing facilities for the cutlery between tasting; a large picture of an open mouth; one copy per child of photocopiable sheet 137, with another at A3 size.

What to do

Explain to the children that they are going to taste a variety of foods and try to describe how something tastes or feels in the mouth. Start by asking the children for appropriate words that they know already, and record these on a large picture of an open mouth.

Now tell the children that they are going to taste some food. They will need to think about how it tastes and feels in their mouths. Tell them that they should not taste any food without asking their parents or guardians. Explain that some children are allergic to certain foods, and it can be dangerous for them to eat even a small amount of these foods.

Opportunities for IT

The children could use a graphing package to display information about different tastes or textures, such as the numbers of foods that were crunchy, sour or juicy.

The work could also be linked to writing about different tastes. The children could use a word processor to write a class poem, or individual poems, about different foods and how they taste. This would enable them to use the new vocabulary they have learned.

Display ideas

Write three or four different words which describe taste and texture on large bubbles coming out of a cartoon mouth. Ask the children to draw, paint or collage different foods which link to these words. Cut out the pictures and mount them in the bubbles.

Reference to photocopiable sheet

Photocopiable sheet 137 can be used to assess children's knowledge of words to describe tastes and textures. It may be appropriate for some children to use pictures rather than words to show the foods that they are tasting.

DESIGN AND TECHNOLOGY

THE NAKED LUNCH   ◆ IDEA

To develop awareness of the structure of a sandwich.

†† *Whole class, working in small groups and/or pairs.*

🕐 *45–60 minutes.*

⚠ *Be aware that some foodstuffs can cause severe reactions in some children. Make sure that the children do not taste the sandwiches after they have been handled. Make sure that the sandwiches are prepared hygienically and stored properly before they are used by the children.*

Previous skills/knowledge needed

It would be useful for the children to have an understanding of correct hygiene procedures when handling food, though reminders should be given before the activity is carried out. It would be useful, but is not essential, for the children to have had experience of working in a small group, using their observation skills and reporting back to others.

Key background information

There are many different types of sandwich, designed in various ways and using various types of bread and fillings. Some fillings are more suitable than others if the sandwich is not to be eaten immediately. This activity need not be expensive if the ingredients are carefully chosen. It is up to you to decide whether the children can eat the sandwiches at the end of the activity, or the sandwiches can be stored properly until the next day, when an activity to evaluate sandwiches could be undertaken.

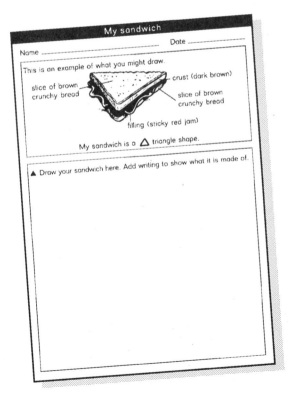

Language to be introduced

sandwich, bread, slice, components, filling, open, texture, smell

shape – square, round, oval, rectangle

types of bread – wholemeal, rye, granary, pitta, soda

size – large, small, bigger, thicker, thinner

Preparation

Check that you have an appropriate word bank prepared, and a book in which to put the children's finished drawings. Copy photocopiable sheet 138 as support for those children who need it.

Resources needed

A collection of sandwiches made from different breads and with different fillings (enough for one sandwich between two or three children), paper towels, a large plastic bag for rubbish, thin plastic gloves (optional), copies of photocopiable sheet 138 (as required).

What to do

At the start of the activity, talk to the whole class about hygienic handling of the sandwiches. Before the children see the sandwiches, ask them for their definition of a sandwich. Illustrate their answers so that all the children can see.

Now provide each group with a plate of three or four different sandwiches. Ask the children not to touch, but to look carefully at the sandwiches. What observations can they make? Allow them a few minutes to talk to each other about their observations. If appropriate, one child could act as a scribe and write down all the ideas.

Ask one child in each group to report back with the group's findings. Relate their answers back to their original definitions. Can other children add to what is being said? Have they noticed the different sizes, shapes, fillings and types of bread? Ask about the texture and the colour. Has anyone talked about the smell?

Ask two or three children to take one sandwich between them and place it on a paper towel. What observations can they make about this sandwich? Tell them they can touch it and take it apart. Allow them a few minutes to talk about what they can see, feel and smell. How was the sandwich made? What are the parts or components? Ask different children to report back on their findings to the whole class, making sure that a range of sandwiches is discussed.

Make a clean space on the table by each child. Now ask the children to draw the sandwich and label the parts, putting in as much detail as possible. The recordings could be stored in a class book shaped like a sandwich.

Suggestion(s) for extension

Ask the children to draw a sandwich from different perspectives: a whole sandwich, a half sandwich, side view, top view.

Encourage the children to research further into sandwiches which are made in other countries, or into the history of the sandwich. What other types of sandwich can they find?

Suggestion(s) for support

There will be peer support, as the children are working in small groups. Offer photocopiable sheet 138 to help with recording. The example on the sheet will give the children ideas about how to draw an annotated picture. Help individual children to focus on particular observations through structured questioning. Write the annotations on the drawings for the children, if necessary.

Assessment opportunities

To build up evidence of achievement, note down comments made by particular children. Write comments on the children's drawings and keep them in a portfolio. Ask a child to draw a sandwich for a friend, or for a particular occasion or celebration. This will provide evidence of the child's understanding of what a sandwich is. If used, the photocopiable sheet will provide additional evidence of this.

Display ideas

Create the outline of a huge sandwich. Get the children to cut out pictures of different types of bread and possible fillings from magazines and leaflets collected from food shops and supermarkets, and stick these on the appropriate parts of the sandwich.

Cut out drawings of different shapes and sizes of bread and fillings. Mount on card and put Velcro or Blu-Tack on the back. The children could create their own giant 2-D sandwiches, using these pictures.

Reference to photocopiable sheet

Photocopiable sheet 138 can be used by children who need support to produce an annotated drawing. It could be used to introduce the idea of annotated drawings.

 SANDWICH FILLINGS ◄IDEA►

To develop understanding that people have different preferences with regard to sandwich fillings. To introduce children to the idea of a survey and its function.

†† *Whole class.*
🕐 *30–45 minutes.*

Previous skills/knowledge needed

The children should have knowledge of sandwiches from taking part in an activity such as the 'The naked lunch' (page 67). It would be useful, but is not essential, for the children to have explored different tastes and textures of food, as in the activity 'Tastes and textures' (page 65).

Key background information

It is important that children realise that not everyone has the same likes and dislikes. When they are making sandwiches at home, there is a need to find out what the family likes and does not like; since there are not many people involved, this information can usually be gathered by asking everyone. However, when a commercial manufacturer makes sandwiches, there are too many people to ask but there is still a need to find out about customer preferences, so a survey is carried out. Information can be gathered through the use of a questionnaire, which can be given over the

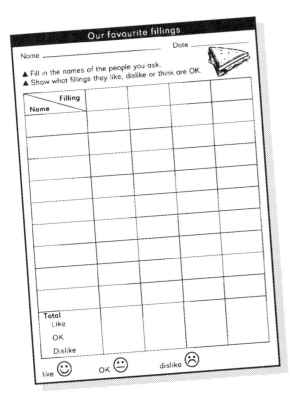

Our favourite fillings

Name _____ Date _____

▲ Fill in the names of the people you ask.
▲ Show what fillings they like, dislike or think are OK.

telephone, through the post or through interviews. This *market research* makes it possible to predict customer preferences.

Language to be introduced

like, dislike, preference, survey, sandwich, need, consumer, customer, questionnaire, filling

Preparation

Check that you have an appropriate word bank prepared, a list of appropriate criteria that you could use to structure the evaluation of the sandwich fillings and an enlarged copy of the chart on photocopiable sheet 139 for your use.

Resources needed

One copy per child of photocopiable sheet 139; an enlarged copy of the photocopiable sheet for use as a recording chart; a selection of fillings, such as jams, spreads and pastes, to look at (optional).

What to do

Ask the children to talk about and investigate sandwich fillings which they have at home. Discuss with the children what sandwich fillings they like and dislike. What is it they like about them? Is it the taste? Perhaps they taste salty, tangy, sweet or crunchy. Perhaps they are allowed to eat them because it is part of a healthy diet. What is it that they dislike about other fillings? Is it that they are bitter or sour, or feel soggy? Ask the children how they could find out which are the most popular sandwich fillings in their class. Discuss the word 'survey' with the children and what it means. They may

have seen people doing surveys of this kind when visiting a supermarket or shopping.

With the children, make a list of the sandwich fillings which they have eaten. Record their preferences on the chart, then ask the children to vote for the one which they like best/least. Then give out photocopiable sheet 139 and ask the children to fill in the sheet, using the information from the chart. They should then fill in the 'Total' boxes at the bottom of the sheet for themselves.

Suggestion(s) for extension

Increase the number of criteria that are used when finding out about preferences, such as the type of bread, the shape, the size, the use of butter or margarine.

The children could take a copy of the blank chart into another class (with the teacher's permission) and find out about the preferences of that class.

Encourage the children to write to different companies (such as Tesco or Boots) for information about how they decide which sandwiches to make. Try making a survey using samples of actual food. The children should think about how to carry it out, the number of flavours to try, making the test fair and how to record the results.

Suggestion(s) for support

As this is a class activity, you can encourage specific children to participate by directing questions to them. The questions can be tightly structured or more open-ended, as necessary.

Assessment opportunities

From the responses which the children give, it will be possible to assess their level of understanding of surveys and the fact that different people have different preferences.

Opportunities for IT

The children could use a simple graphing package to display the results of their class surveys of popular/unpopular sandwich fillings or types of bread.

Alternatively, they could use a database to record the information about each child's preference. The fieldnames for the database might include:

name	Sally
sex	girl
favourite bread	white sliced
least favourite bread	brown granary
favourite filling	eggs
least favourite filling	peanut butter

The database could be used to see how many children prefer white or brown bread, or sorted to see which is the most popular filling. Comparisons could also be made between boys and girls. The data could also be used to plot graphs and pie charts representing preferences.

Display ideas

Display the children's pictures of their favourite sandwiches. Allow them to use a range of media (collage in fabric or cut-out pictures, pastels, pencil, paint) to create these pictures. Display the charts of the children's preferences, alongside the conclusions drawn from the data they have collected. Use a database to store information, and print out findings in the form of a graph or pie chart.

Reference to photocopiable sheet

Photocopiable sheet 139 can be used to show how information needs to be put into a chart so that conclusions can be made more easily. It can be used as support for some children, or as an introduction to the systematic recording of data by the whole class. Fill in the top part of the chart with the children; then leave them to total the numbers in the bottom boxes.

MAKING BUNS ◆ FPT

To develop practical skills including the ability to combine and weigh ingredients. To develop an understanding of the need to follow instructions from a recipe.

†† *Small group.*

🕐 *60 minutes.*

⚠ *Make sure that all the children are aware of, and put into practice, safety and hygiene rules. Make sure that no-one is able to touch the hot oven.*

Previous skills/knowledge needed

It is essential that the children have an appropriate knowledge and understanding of safety and hygiene when working with food and heat. It would be useful, but is not essential, for

Making buns

For a small group of children.
You need:

soft butter or margarine · 1 egg · sugar · self-raising flour
measuring cup · or · scales · plastic mixing bowl · small plastic container
fork · spoon · teaspoon · knife · sieve
paper cases · baking tray · cooling tray · oven gloves

1. Preheat oven to Gas Mark 5 (375°F/190°C).
2. Weigh out 55g butter or margarine and 55g sugar, and put them in the mixing bowl.
3. Cream together until almost white.
4. Crack the egg into a small plastic container, then add to the mixture.
5. Mix smoothly, with a circular movement.
6. Weigh out 55g flour and add to the mixture.
7. Mix until the mixture is creamy and smooth.
8. Put a large teaspoonful of the mixture into each paper case.
9. Put in the oven for about 15 minutes.
10. Let an adult take the buns out of the oven and put them on a cooling tray.
11. Do **not** touch until cool.

them to have had experience of weighing, using non-standard or standard measures and following instructions.

Key background information

It is important that through a step-by-step approach, children are led to understand the need to follow a recipe in order to produce the desired end product. When mixed together, food ingredients combine and change consistency; they change again when heated. The correct safety and hygiene procedures must be carried out at all times.

Language to be introduced

bun, mix, cake, ingredient, combine, paper case, flour, egg, butter, sugar, beat, heat, cooling tray, baking tray, oven, oven glove, sieve, scales

Preparation

Check that the oven will be available when needed. Make sure that any adult involved is clear about the purpose of the activity and the importance of the children's involvement during the preparation, at all stages of the making and during the clearing away. Copy photocopiable sheet 140 as a recipe card for the children to use; cover it in plastic to keep it clean. Preheat the oven to Gas Mark 5 (375°F/190°C).

Resources needed

A table and plastic covering, a disinfectant spray and cloth, access to a preheated oven, recipe cards (copied from photocopiable sheet 140), scales or a measuring cup, ingredients for 6–7 buns (55g soft butter or margarine, 55g sugar, 1 egg, 55g self-raising flour), plastic mixing bowls, forks, spoons, sieves, paper cases, baking trays, cooling

trays, blunt knives, oven gloves, washing-up facilities, drying-up cloths, ready-made buns or a picture (optional).

What to do

First remind the children about the safety and hygiene rules, similar to those outlined in the activity 'Do it clean' (page 64). Discuss the ingredients and equipment that are on display. Can the children name them? Explain that they are going to use the ingredients to make small cakes or buns. If necessary, provide a bun (or an illustration of one) for the children to look at. Talk with them about the need to follow a recipe, so that they know what to use and what to do. When they are working with the food, check that they look at the recipe card at every stage; ask them recurrently what they need to do next. Let the children take turns to carry out the tasks. Explain the need to preheat the oven so that the mixture goes in at the right temperature.

The children should weigh the butter and then the sugar before putting them into the mixing bowl. What tool will they use to combine and cream the two ingredients? Encourage them to cream the butter and sugar in a circular movement in the bowl, until the mixture is smooth and creamy. What changes do they observe? If necessary, remind the children that putting their fingers into the mixture is not hygienic.

Next, they should decide how to crack the egg. They should crack it into a small container, in case bits of shell get in with the egg. Then they add the egg to the mixture. Again, encourage the children to mix it in smoothly with a circular movement.

Now ask the children to weigh and sieve the flour. Why do they need to sieve it? Add the flour to the mixing bowl and mix it in until the mixture is smooth and creamy. Put paper cases in the baking tray and spoon some mixture into each case. Put in the oven for about 15–20 minutes. Do check the cooking process, as the heat in ovens can vary. An adult will need to take the tray out of the oven and leave it to cool.

When the buns have cooled down, the children can take them out of the baking tray and leave them on the cooling tray until they are quite cold. Can the children describe all the changes that have happened? Do the buns look good enough to eat? Tasting the end product can take place later in the day. The children can each have a piece to try. What does it taste like? Is it fluffy inside? Can they suggest any flavour that they might add to improve the taste?

Suggestion(s) for extension

The children could create a new recipe, or one with imaginary ingredients, and write a recipe card. They could carry out their own survey into which type of cake is most popular among their friends or family.

Suggestion(s) for support

Some children may need help from an adult or peer to follow the instructions correctly, or to combine the ingredients. They could use non-standard measures.

Assessment opportunities

Note those children who understand the need to follow the recipe instructions; those who can weigh accurately; and those who can combine the ingredients successfully.

Opportunities for IT

The children could use a word processor or desktop publishing package to create a recipe card. They could also add pictures created using an art package, scanned from their own line drawings or taken from collections of clip art.

Display ideas

Make a large-sized recipe card. Using drawings (with or without annotations), the children can work individually or in pairs to draw/write each step of the recipe. Decorate the card with drawings or paintings of the buns, or ask a child to make a print block and print buns around the card.

Reference to photocopiable sheet

Photocopiable sheet 140 can be copied onto card and used by the children as a recipe for making the buns.

GOOD ENOUGH TO EAT FPT

To understand the importance of the visual presentation of food.

Class or group, then individual work.

60 minutes.

The children should not taste the Plasticine or salt dough.

Key background information

The appearance of food affects our judgement of it. We are likely to prefer food which looks attractive, care having been taken over such features as colour, shape and texture.

DESIGN AND TECHNOLOGY

Language to be introduced

colour, shape, shade, round, circular, oval, square, rectangular, triangular, size, small, large, cut, texture, mould

Preparation

Collect a variety of sweets, unwrap them, place them on a plate and cover them. Include a range of shapes, sizes, colours and textures, and sweets for different purposes or occasions. Make the salt dough (if appropriate) by mixing equal quantities of flour and salt, then adding just enough water to form a cohesive mass. The quantity needed will depend on whether the activity is carried out by a class or a group.

Resources needed

A collection of different sweets, some of which can be unwrapped; different-shaped paper/plastic plates; box tops or other food containers cut from thin card or paper; a variety of different-coloured pieces of salt dough, modelling material or Plasticine; rolling pins, different-shaped cutters, plastic knives; a board or chart for writing.

What to do

Start by asking the children what makes them want to eat a certain food when they look at it. Record their ideas on a board or large sheet of paper. Then uncover the collection of sweets and ask the children to look carefully at them. What do they like about the look of particular sweets? Is it their shape, size, colour, texture? Encourage them to use specific vocabulary such as *rectangular*, *circular*, *smooth*, *brittle*. Refer back to their ideas about why food looks attractive.

Ask them to think about sweets which they do *not* think look nice. What are their reasons for feeling this? Remind them, if necessary, that you are *not* asking for ideas about taste and smell. Try to extend their reasons from 'It's nice' or 'I like it' to a judgement such as 'The colour is like mud and I don't want to put it in my mouth.'

For what situation or people are the sweets appropriate? For example: a heart-shaped sweet for Valentine's day, a chocolate as a special gift, a smooth round-shaped sweet for someone with a sore throat. Talk to the children about design, and how the makers of sweets think about all these factors in order to create an appropriate product that will sell.

Tell the children that they are going to design sweets using a modelling material. Why do they think they are not going to use real food? (Think about how much food would be wasted.) You can give them a special purpose for the sweets, or they can choose their own. Purposes could include a birthday present for a particular person, or a special gathering such as a Christmas party. Let the children work on their own with the modelling material to design sweets. They can roll out, cut, shape and choose the colour of their material. Ask them to display their model sweets on a piece of shaped card, or in a small box of their choice. Next, have a class discussion about the model sweets. Ask the children to explain the purposes of their sweets. Do they think that the sweets are appropriate for the purpose? (Obviously, this discussion will need to be handled sensitively.)

Suggestion(s) for extension

Ask the children to cut out pictures of different foods from magazines, labels and food advertisements. Give them each a paper plate (or get them to cut one out from card) and ask them to create a meal that looks attractive by sticking pictures of different foods onto the plate. They could create a 3-D model of a plate of food, using a variety of different types of paper, card and reclaimed materials.

Suggestion(s) for support

Direct specific questions to those children who do not take part in the discussion. Encourage them to give reasons why they like/dislike the look of the sweets. Some children may need help with cutting, shaping and rolling and deciding on a purpose for their sweets.

Assessment opportunities

Note the children who make suggestions about why food looks attractive and give reasons for their answers. The finished products will provide evidence of individual achievement in designing. Some of the finished products could be photographed, annotated to indicate the level at which the child is working and kept in a school portfolio.

Opportunities for IT

The children could use an art package to create their own design for an attractive sweet or a plate of food. Framework software such as 'My World 2' could be used with the 'Food' file to design a plate of food, a pizza topping or a sandwich.

Display ideas

Cut out two very large sweet containers. Label them 'Good enough to eat' and 'Would you want to eat this?' Add a smiley face to one container and a sad face to the other. Get the children to draw sweets, cut them out and stick them onto the appropriate container.

Make a teaching display to remind the children of some of the criteria which they need to think about when evaluating the appearance of food. Under the heading 'What makes food look good?' put up words such as *colour*, *shape*, *size* and *texture* made from large letters. Ask the children to add pictures, cut out from magazines, which show good use of these qualities.

Construction kits

This section of the book contains IDEAs and FPTs relating to the use of construction kits in design and technology. Construction kits can be used in a variety of ways. Before the children can start to work on focused tasks, they will need some free play in which to explore the kits for themselves. The kits can then be used (for example) for evaluation, for investigation, for modelling and to demonstrate a particular concept (such as axles and wheels).

Through working with construction kits, the children will have the opportunity to gain knowledge and understanding relating to structures (such as the concept of stability) and mechanisms (such as wheels, axles, levers, pulleys and moving joints). The skills which the children will develop include modelling, imagining, following instructions, evaluating, investigating, planning, drawing, manipulating and working independently and with others.

The following contexts are particularly appropriate for work with construction kits: houses and homes, shelter, the playground, the fairground, transport and movement.

WHEEL LIFE ◆ IDEA

To investigate the movement of wheels and their attachment to a chassis. To create something that moves on wheels. To develop the children's ability to disassemble and reassemble.

†† *Large or small group, working in pairs.*

⏱ *45 minutes.*

Previous skills/knowledge needed

This activity could be linked to 'Coming apart' in the 'Mechanisms' chapter (page 27).

Key background information

To make something move on wheels, either the wheels can be fitted tightly onto an axle so that the axle turns and the wheels move with it, or the axle can be fitted tightly onto the chassis and the wheels remain free to turn round. A stopper on each end of the axle may be needed to prevent the wheels from falling off it. Wheels that are bolted onto the side of a chassis will not be able to turn round.

Language to be introduced

axle, chassis, wheel

Preparation

Provide construction kits with wheels and axles, and decide how many pairs of children can use them at any one time. Decide on the pairs that should work together (if the children are not deciding for themselves), and whether you or they will decide who records and who makes. Make two or three models from a construction kit, each with a different number of wheels.

Resources needed

One or more construction kits with axles and wheels; two or three models with wheels; one copy of photocopiable sheet 141 for each pair; writing materials.

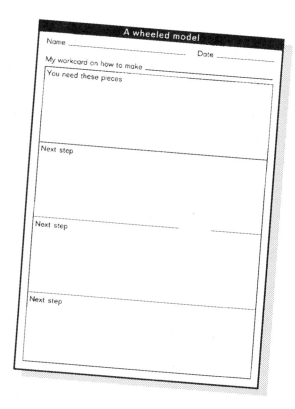

A wheeled model

Name _____

Date _____

My workcard on how to make _____

You need these pieces

Next step

Next step

Next step

What to do

To provide a context for investigating wheels and axles, collect (through discussion) the children's ideas about objects that move on wheels. Their suggestions could then be sorted into objects which have one, two, three and four wheels. Show the children the models, made from construction kits, with different numbers of wheels. Check that they know the terms *axle*, *wheel* and *chassis*. Through discussion of the models, help the children to understand that whatever the number of wheels, they need an axle; and that if wheels are to move round, they cannot be fixed onto the side of an object so they cannot turn.

Tell the children that they are going to make something with wheels, and then they are going to produce a step-by-

DESIGN AND TECHNOLOGY

step guide for someone else to help them make the same model. Give them photocopiable sheet 141 and explain how they will use it. If appropriate, you could work through an example using a model which you have made. In the first box on the sheet, the children should draw all the pieces which someone would need to make the finished product. The children should make their model first and check that it works. Then they should disassemble it and, as they put it together again, draw pictures to show how they are reassembling it. Explain that they can use the other side of the paper if they do not have enough boxes on the first side. Allow the children time to talk with each other, making sure that they have a clear idea of what they are going to make. Remind the children while they are completing the photocopiable sheet that they need to draw in every stage of the making process. The children can try out each others' cards to check that everyone has made a vehicle with wheels that move.

Suggestion(s) for extension

The children can make other models with different numbers of wheels. How can they fit on odd numbers of wheels and still make the vehicle balance?

Suggestion(s) for support

Careful pairing of the children will allow them to support each other. Individual children may need to check each step with an adult before they draw it. Further discussion about how axles and wheels function may be needed.

Assessment opportunities

Observation of the children's modelling work makes it possible to assess their understanding of the workings of wheels and axles. From their modelling work and their recording on photocopiable sheet 141, it will be possible to assess the children's ability to disassemble and assemble an object with wheels.

Opportunities for IT

The children could use a word processor to write their own set of instructions for assembling a wheeled object. They could add simple pictures drawn using an art or drawing package.

A drawing package such as 'Picture IT' (from Appian Way) or a framework package such as 'My World 2' could be used with a bank of suitable construction kit parts which match those being used, so that the children can redraw their model on the computer.

Display ideas

Put some of the completed photocopiable sheets in plastic wallets to preserve them, and display them alongside some of the finished models. Leave out a construction kit, so that the children can try out the sheets for themselves.

Reference to photocopiable sheet

Give a copy of photocopiable sheet 141 to each pair after they have completed their model. Remind them to draw all the pieces that are needed to make their model in the first box and then to go one step at a time, recording the steps in consecutive boxes. Confirm with each pair who records and who makes the model.

EVALUATING A CONSTRUCTION KIT
IDEA

To develop the children's ability to make judgements about a product. To develop the children's ability to work co-operatively.

†† *Small group or pairs.*

🕐 *45 minutes.*

Previous skills/knowledge needed

This activity links with others which focus on evaluation, such as 'Useful things' (page 95), 'The right hat' (page 54) and 'A popular package' (page 41).

Key background information

While adults may have evaluated the construction kits in the school, the children's viewpoint is often overlooked. Children can often see possibilities which are missed by adults, who may have preconceived ideas about what the kit can and cannot be used for. It is thus important that any framework gives the children the opportunity to comment on the kit.

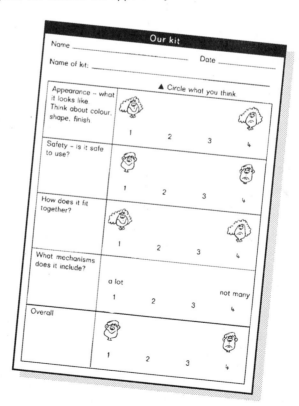

Construction kits

Language to be introduced

evaluation, appearance, construction kit, shape, finish, mechanism

Preparation

Make sure that the children have experienced free play with the kit in order to become familiar with it. Decide whether the children are going to work in pairs or in a small group (about four).

Resources needed

One construction kit and one copy of photocopiable sheet 142 for each pair or group.

What to do

Display the kit so that the children can see all the pieces (or a range of pieces). It is important that the evaluation has a structure, so that the children are encouraged to move beyond saying that they like it or do not like it. Talk about appearance in terms of colour, the different shapes that are used, the material the kit is made from and the finish on the different parts. Discuss how easily the parts fit together and can be taken apart. Ask the children to see what parts there are which, when fitted into a model, will allow the model to move. These might include a turntable, wheels, axles and hinges. Ask the children whether they are able to make many different models or are limited by the pieces in the kit. Discuss how safe the kit is to use, and whether there are some pieces that are sharp or very small.

Next, give out copies of photocopiable sheet 142 and explain to the children that they are going to make a survey of the construction kit, giving their opinions about it. Check that they understand what they have to do and how to fill in the sheet. When they have completed the sheet, carry out a whole-class discussion about what the kit's good points are and what changes, if any, the children would make to improve it.

Suggestion(s) for extension

The children can carry out this activity with all the construction kits in the school and create a book for reference purposes. Others can then use this book to find out which kit would be most suitable for the project on which they are working.

Suggestion(s) for support

Questions may need to be directed towards individual children to make sure that they have understood the idea behind the activity. They may need more closed questions initially, to help them focus on specific aspects of the kit, before the discussion is opened up.

Assessment opportunities

From listening to individual comments and looking at the completed photocopiable sheets, it is possible to assess the children's ability to evaluate and make decisions about the quality and usefulness of a product.

Opportunities for IT

The children could use a word processor or desktop publishing package to write and redraft their evaluations. These could be printed out and mounted to make a book.

A more ambitious project would be to use a multi-media authoring package to create an electronic presentation of the evaluations. This type of presentation allows children to combine different forms of information, including text written on a word processor and pictures drawn with an art or drawing package, scanned from the children's own line drawings or manufacturers' literature about the construction kit or taken from clipart collections. The children can even add their own voices, recorded using a microphone attached to the computer.

A list of the different construction kits could be used as a title page for this project, so that when the child clicked on a picture of a LEGO block he or she would be taken to a set of linked pages about LEGO. This set might include the children's recorded voices describing the kit, pictures of the different blocks and the types of model that could be made, and other information gathered in the evaluation. An arrow or other picture (icon) would then take the child back to the main title page.

The children could work in small groups, each group designing the pages for one construction kit. This type of software requires extra support, especially when it is being used for the first time with younger children, and is best undertaken when additional classroom help is available.

Display ideas

Mount photographs of construction kit models, or some of the pictures which come with a kit, and display them with questions (written on strips of card) about the kit, such as *What different pieces are there which could be used to make a model move? Are the pieces easy to put together? Are the shapes well-made?* Add some of the complete photocopiable sheets to the display.

DESIGN AND TECHNOLOGY

Reference to photocopiable sheet

Give out the sheet after the initial discussion. Go over the headings with the children and help them to decide who will fill it in. Remind them how important it is to put in reasons for their likes and dislikes, such as *We like the bright colours because they make the finished model look exciting.*

A CLIMBING FRAME ◆ FPT

To develop understanding of stability. To develop the practical ability to join materials in different ways. To develop the children's ability to evaluate their own products.

†† *Small group, working in pairs.*

🕑 *60 minutes.*

Previous skills/knowledge needed

This activity links with activities in the 'Structures' chapter which relate to stability.

Key background information

Climbing frames are an appropriate context for introductory work on the concept of stability, as many children will have had personal experience of them and will thus be aware of the importance of stability in this structure. The children need to understand that a wide base and a frame which balances on legs of the same length help stability. When they are looking at their finished model, the children need to accept that improvements can sometimes be made. Their model may satisfy some, but not all, of the criteria set at the beginning of the task.

Language to be introduced

climbing frame, stability, safety, shape, curved, straight, support, balance

Preparation

If possible, take the children to a park or show them a video which has a climbing frame in it. Cut out a selection of climbing frames from catalogues and mount them on a poster, ready to show the children. Make a climbing frame which is *not* stable from a construction kit.

Resources needed

A poster of climbing frames, a model climbing frame, construction kits.

What to do

Talk with the children about climbing frames that they have seen. Show them the poster of different frames. During the discussion, try to emphasise the importance of stability and safety, as well as challenge, when designing a climbing frame. Now show them the model climbing frame which you have made. Ask them how the pieces fit together, what makes the frame stand up and why some parts may be unstable or wobbly. Emphasise the need for a wide base to make the frame stable.

Give the children time to work in pairs, making a frame. Remind them that the frame should be interesting to climb, it should stand up and it should be safe (with no pieces jutting out). When the frames are finished, take each criterion in turn and ask the children to decide which frames they find interesting, which are the most stable and which are safe. Encourage them to give reasons for their judgements. If appropriate, the children could modify their frames following this discussion.

Suggestion(s) for extension

The children could look at pictures of building sites with scaffolding frames. How are these made, and what are they used for? What safety precautions are taken?

Suggestion(s) for support

Careful pairing of the children will allow for peer support. Some children may need to make a number of models before they can see what is needed to make something stable.

Assessment opportunities

During the discussion and making, it will be possible to identify children who have an understanding of what is needed for stability.

Opportunities for IT

The children could use framework software such as 'My World 2' with the T & D 'Recreation' file to extend this activity by planning their own play area.

Display ideas

Display the children's finished frames together with the poster of frames from catalogues. Add a caption such as 'What are the similarities and differences between the pictures and our models?'

A RIGID SHAPE — FPT

To develop understanding of rigid shapes and their importance in supporting structures.

†† *Large or small group.*

⏲ *30–45 minutes.*

Key background information

The triangle is the only straight-edged shape that is rigid. Other shapes, such as squares and rectangles, can be made rigid by adding a strip across them (see Figure 1).

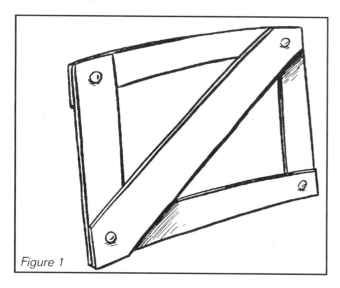

Figure 1

When the children are making shapes, check that their strips are not flexible. If they are, the children will still be unable to push the triangle out of shape; but they will be able to bend it, thus distorting the shape. A roof is one of the most common places where children can see that triangles have been used.

Language to be introduced

rigid, triangular, square, circular, rectangular

Preparation

If appropriate, the children could go on a 'looking walk' to see what shapes they can find before they take part in this activity. Collect stiff strips that can be fixed together to make different shapes. The strips should have holes in. Geostrips (plastic) or Briomec (wood) could be used; or you could make your own from very stiff card. Provide enough paper fasteners for the children to use. Find pictures of objects and buildings which illustrate the use of triangles for support.

Resources needed

Strips with holes in, paper fasteners, pictures which illustrate the structural use of triangular shapes.

What to do

Tell the children that they are going to investigate shapes to find which ones are rigid. Talk to the children about the word *rigid*, and explain that it means something which is very stiff and cannot be bent. This is particularly important when an architect is designing a building. The building will be no use if it falls down because the architect has not used a rigid shape. Ask the children to suggest rigid shapes, and to give reasons for their suggestions. Then ask the children if they can think of anywhere in the school building, their homes or the buildings near the school where triangles have been used. If a picture of the frame of a roof (or something similar) is available, show the children this to reinforce the idea. Link any appropriate suggestions to the rest of the activity.

Show the children each of the shapes shown in Figure 2, in turn. Move each shape and discuss with the children what happens. Lay the shapes on a flat surface, so that you can push the shape but not bend it. It is important that they see that the triangle is a rigid shape and thus it is important to use this shape in buildings (for example). Put out the strips and the brass paper fasteners, and allow the children time to make different shapes and test them. Ask them to draw a rigid and a non-rigid shape and to label them.

Suggestion(s) for extension

The children could design patterns using triangles, then construct triangular frames using Constructo straws or something similar.

DESIGN AND TECHNOLOGY

INVESTIGATING A CONSTRUCTION KIT

IDEA

To develop the children's understanding of a construction kit through investigation. To develop the children's ability to form mental images.

†† *Small group.*

⏲ *45 minutes.*

They could continue to collect examples of the use of triangles in buildings, and record their findings through drawings that focus on how triangular structures are adapted (for instance in archways or bridges). They may like to try to find ways of making a non-rigid shape, such as a square, rigid.

Suggestion(s) for support
Some children may need further opportunities to play with the strips in order to develop their understanding of rigid shapes.

Assessment opportunities
From discussion with individual children and from their recording, it will be possible to assess their ideas about rigidity.

Opportunities for IT
The children could design their own triangle patterns using an art or drawing program. They should be shown how to create, resize and move the triangles, rotate and flip them, fill them with colours and change (or even create) the colour or pattern to fill the triangles.

Display ideas
Put up the pictures and photographs which show the use of triangles in construction. Make large shapes which are not rigid and a triangle which is. Add captions such as *Which shape is rigid? Can you make a non-rigid shape rigid?*

Previous skills/knowledge needed
Links can be made with other activities which develop drawing and modelling skills, such as 'Hard paper' (page 103), 'A popular package' (page 41) and 'A thumb pot' (page 100).

Key background information
The development of modelling and drawing skills can be overlooked; it is important that children are taught these skills at an early stage of developing design and technology capability, in parallel with their making skills. Asking the children to imagine what model they can make from construction materials gives them an opportunity to form a mental image of how these materials might fit together. A good understanding of how things fit together and combine to work will help the children to develop their ability to draw a 3-D model. Encourage the children to use different drawing techniques, such as shading and sketching, to produce the effect of a 3-D drawing.

Language to be introduced
image, 3-D, sketch, shade

Preparation
Decide how many pieces you will select for the children to use in making something simple – probably four or five pieces. If possible, include pieces which fit together in different ways. Then select the pieces and make a model with them. Disassemble it ready for the activity. Collect enough plastic covers for the completed activity sheets.

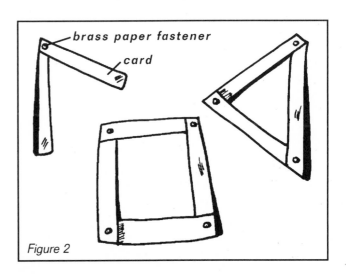

brass paper fastener
card

Figure 2

DESIGN AND TECHNOLOGY

Resources needed

A construction kit, plastic covers, lead pencils, blank paper.

What to do

Lay the selected pieces of the construction kit on a table, so that the children can see them. Ask the children to describe each piece, thinking about shape, size, finish, what the piece can do and what it could be used for. It may be able to turn round, move up and down, or support other pieces. Before you start to put the pieces together, ask the children if they can imagine what could be made with the pieces. Encourage them to 'see' in their minds different ways of arranging the pieces. Then fit the pieces together slowly, one at a time. Ask the children to describe how the pieces fit together. They may slot, click or push. Look at the finished model. Ask the children what has been made and if it is similar to what they imagined.

Give out some blank sheets of paper. Explain to the children that they are going to choose their own pieces and then draw them carefully on the sheet. They will then construct their model and, using a lead pencil, draw what they have made. Remind them to look carefully all the time, and to produce drawings which show the 3-D nature of the pieces. They may need to shade the drawing to indicate depth. Finally, they could try swapping their completed sheets and making each others' models from the drawings. Remind them to keep their sheets in plastic covers for protection.

Suggestion(s) for extension

Tell the children that they are going to make something of their own choice (linked to a class topic). Ask them to draw what their model will look like before making it, then draw what it does look like after making it. They can highlight any differences.

Suggestion(s) for support

The children may need individual support to fit the pieces together.

Some children could start by drawing just one piece of the construction kit in 3-D form.

Assessment opportunities

It is possible to assess the children's ability to form mental images from the suggestions that they make before the pieces of the kit are fitted together. From their drawings, their ability to make a 3-D drawing of a model can be assessed.

Display ideas

Display some of the finished models together with the drawings. Keep changing the models and drawings to stimulate interest. Include more complex models – or pictures of them – and relate these to 'real' constructions such as buildings or machines.

WHAT CAN IT DO? IDEA

To develop the children's investigative skills. To extend their understanding of mechanisms.
†† Small group, working individually or in pairs.
🕑 45 minutes.

Previous skills/knowledge needed

The children will need to have experiencedsome unstructured play with the kit in order to be familiar with the pieces and how they fit together. They will need to have some knowledge of mechanisms, which could be gained through activities in the 'Mechanisms' chapter.

Key background information

While the children are investigating the new kit (that is, new to them), make sure that no one person is 'taking over' the session. It has been shown that boys can dominate in situations such as this, so single-gender groups or individual work may need to be considered for this activity. The children need to investigate how the pieces fit together, as well as what each piece can do. It is not possible to specify here which mechanisms the children should investigate, as this will vary from kit to kit. However, the framework of this activity is equally appropriate to use when any mechanism (or any new concept) is to be introduced.

Language to be introduced

construction kit, mechanism, fit together, slot, click, push

Preparation

Unpack the 'new' kit and check that you are familiar with how the pieces fit together, whether there are specific ways of putting the kit back into its container and what some of the main features of the kit are (such as the mechanisms). Decide how many children can work with the kit at any one time, who will be in the group and whether the children are to work individually or in pairs. Find a drawing tool to make a thick line which can be seen by a group of children.

Resources needed

A construction kit, a large sheet of paper and a thick drawing tool (such as a thick black pencil), pencils and paper for the children.

What to do

Put out the kit so that the whole group can see it (preferably on the floor in a carpeted area). The children will already have played with the kit. Ask them how many ways they have found of fitting the pieces together. They may suggest slot, push and click. Quickly sketch these on a large chart, so that everyone can see.

Ask what they have already been able to make with the pieces that has a moving part in it. Again, sketch these quickly

DESIGN AND TECHNOLOGY

on a large chart so that everyone can see. Ask individual children to pick up any parts that, when put together with others, will allow movement. These might include wheels, pulleys, linkages (to make levers), joiners and turntables. Demonstrate and sketch any which the children miss. Discuss the different types of movement which each mechanism makes – up and down, round and round, backwards and forwards.

Now ask the children to make a model with a part that moves. They can write a label for it, to explain what parts they have used and what the mechanism is called.

Suggestion(s) for extension
Allow the children to make models with different mechanisms. Over a period of time, ask the children to make sketches of mechanisms which they see in everyday life, and to collect pictures of them. These can be compiled as a class book of mechanisms.

Suggestion(s) for support
Further discussion may be needed with individual children, to help them identify pieces of the kit that will make a mechanism and how these can be fitted together.

Assessment opportunities
From observation of the children working with the kit and from their finished models, their ability to put together a construction kit and their understanding of a particular mechanism can be assessed.

Opportunities for IT
The children could use a word processor or desktop publishing package to write and print labels to go with their displayed model. They could experiment with different fonts and styles to make the labels more interesting. They might also add a simple border. If they use an A4 page layout for the labels, the printed page can be folded so that it stands up on its own next to the model. However, the children will need to investigate where to write the text for the labels so that they are in the right places and are the right way up when the label is printed out and folded!

Display ideas
Display the models together with the children's labels. These can be changed frequently, so that others have the opportunity to make new models with the same kit. Keep a book by the display; when the models are broken up, stick the labels in the book to provide reference material for all the children.

ONE STEP AT A TIME
To develop the children's ability to follow instructions.
†† *Large or small group, working in pairs.*
🕑 *60 minutes.*

Key background information
It is important that children learn the importance of planning out the making process. By using this step-by-step approach to building a model, they should begin to see the importance of working through instructions in the correct order. This will help them when they come to make models from other materials which are less easily taken apart. For example, it is difficult to fit a straw axle through a box if the wheels have been secured to the axle first.

DESIGN AND TECHNOLOGY

Language to be introduced

construction kit, plan, sequence, step-by-step, workcard

Preparation

Check that the kit has enough pieces for the children to use, and that appropriate workcards or worksheets are available. It may be appropriate to use more than one kit, and to put the cards in a plastic cover to protect them.

Resources needed

One or more construction kits, with accompanying cards or worksheets.

What to do

Group the children in pairs around the kit. Put out the cards or worksheets that accompany the kit on a table, and ask the children to look at them and to select one which they would like to use. Make sure that the pictures/instructions on each card are clear, and that it is possible to make a model using them with the kit. Check that the children do want the particular card they have chosen, as it is important that they make something that interests them. Ask them how they think that it will be best for each pair to tackle the problem. They may suggest taking turns to find a piece, each child doing one step at a time, or the pair making each model together.

Discuss with them the importance of having a plan and thinking about a sequence, so that they do not just take pieces and try putting them anywhere. It may be that they put out all the pieces they think they will need, arrange them in the order they think they will need them and then take turns putting them together.

Let them make their models, but ask them to remember how they planned out and sequenced the task. Give them a set amount of time (whatever you feel is appropriate) and then ask them to stop. Look at the models and ask different pairs to describe what they have made and how they set about the task. Can they say what problems might have arisen if they had not followed the instructions correctly?

Suggestion(s) for extension

The children could make suggestions about anything they would change on the cards to help them make the model more easily.

The children could design and make their own model, then create a step-by-step guide to the making process for others to follow.

Suggestions for support

Peer support can be useful if the children are paired appropriately. It may be necessary to work with individuals and pairs to plan each step and then leave the children to fit the pieces together on their own. The teacher can choose a card to match the children's expected level of ability.

Assessment opportunities

From observation of the way in which the children work, and from their comments about how they have made their model, it is possible to assess their ability to understand and follow instructions when carrying out a task.

Opportunities for IT

The children could use a word processor to write and edit the sequence of instructions for making their model. They can use the 'cut and paste' or 'drag and drop' facility to help them put instructions into the correct sequence. The completed set of instructions could be printed out and given to another group of children, to see if they can follow the instructions and make the same model (out of the same construction kit).

Display ideas

Make a display of the finished models together with the appropriate instruction cards. Update this display regularly as the children work on model-making. If they draw or write out any modifications to the cards, these can be added to the display. Leave one card in the centre, together with the pieces needed to make up the model shown. Leave a 'comments' book by the side, so that the children can write down their suggestions for possible amendments to the card.

DESIGN AND TECHNOLOGY

Electricity

This section of the book contains IDEAs and FPTs relating to electrical circuits and switches. While electrical circuits are not included in the programme of study for design and technology at Key Stage 1, they are included in the programme of study for science; many children towards the end of Key Stage 1 are using circuits in the products which they make.

Through the activities in this chapter, the children will have opportunities to gain knowledge and understanding relating to the construction of a simple circuit, including a light bulb and a switch. The work builds on that covered in science activities, but focuses on the application of knowledge and skills relating to the making and use of circuits and switches, which can then be incorporated into products which the children make; and to the potential dangers of electricity.

The skills which the children will gain include evaluating commercial products, assessing their fitness for their purpose, co-operating with each other and following instructions.

The following contexts are particularly appropriate for work with electricity: games, stories, homes, houses and transport.

DESIGN AND
TECHNOLOGY

DETECTIVE WORK

IDEA

To investigate what components are needed to make a circuit. To explore, through disassembly, how components are put together to make a circuit. To work together co-operatively. To talk to an audience and listen to others.

†† *Large or small group, working in pairs.*

🕐 *45 minutes.*

⚠ *Make the children aware that they should not disassemble electrical goods or plugs unless supervised by an adult. A battery-operated object is not the same as one powered from mains electricity! Explain the dangers of plugs and main electricity, and the need for safe handling and disposal of batteries.*

Key background information

This work can be linked to the science curriculum. Children need an understanding of how a circuit and a switch work before they can apply this knowledge and incorporate it into a made product. They should begin to understand that there must be a complete circuit for a bulb to light, and that a switch can be used to break the circuit and thus turn off the light. A torch is one of the most useful items to disassemble as it is easy to take apart and put together, it is within the children's experience and it is relatively cheap to buy as a school resource. Some suppliers now make see-through torches, so that the parts can be seen more easily. Other battery-operated items could be used for this activity.

Language to be introduced

electricity, bulb, circuit, holder, discover, battery, holder, wire, connection, detective

Preparation

Decide on appropriate pairs, based (for example) on friendships or on ability with writing. Gather props to turn the pairs into detectives (hat, pipe, glasses, coat or jacket) for their presentation to the others.

Resources needed

One torch per pair of children, a small screwdriver (if necessary), props for detectives, paper and pencils.

What to do

Give a torch to each pair of children, and explain that they are going to be detectives. They should find out as much as they can about the torch in a given time. The children can take the torch apart carefully, but they must remember how to put it back together. Decide what amount of time is appropriate, and encourage them to record their findings on paper. They may draw individual pieces (such as the switch or the battery) in isolation, or draw diagrams relating different parts to each other (such as the switch and the bulb). This should help them with a more systematic approach to their detection.

While the children are disassembling and investigating, ask them questions to direct their attention to the different parts they can find and how they fit together. Why do they think the bulb lights? Use the correct vocabulary when talking with the children. Now ask them to switch on their torches to check that the bulb lights.

When they have had enough time, ask a selection of pairs to report back on their findings. Draw out in discussion the need for a complete circuit including batteries, a bulb, connections and a switch. Encourage the children to listen to each other and to ask questions. Encourage the 'detectives' to take turns in reporting and to speak clearly, giving evidence for their conclusions.

Suggestion(s) for extension

The children could disassemble a range of battery-operated items which have different circuits, identify similarities and differences, and make up a presentation about these devices and how they work. Encourage more able children to think about how detectives and scientists look for evidence to answer a question.

Suggestion(s) for support

If the pairs are chosen carefully, the children should be able to support each other in most respects. Questions about the parts and how they fit together in a circuit may need to be asked to help some children clarify their understanding of circuits.

DESIGN AND TECHNOLOGY

Electricity

Assessment opportunities

From the written evidence and the children's comments during the investigation, it will be possible to assess the children's understanding of circuits and how a switch works. As they work together and make their presentation, you can assess their ability to work co-operatively, to speak to an audience and to listen to other children.

Opportunities for IT

The children could use a word processor to write and redraft their presentations. The set of presentations could be bound to make a class book for others to read. Children could add pictures to their writing, drawn using a graphics package or scanned from their own line drawings.

Display ideas

Mount some of the children's 'detective notebook' sheets. Make some of their main findings into posters. Leave one or two of the torches on display for the children to continue to investigate and disassemble.

MAKING A CIRCUIT ◆IDEA▶

To construct an electrical circuit. To work together co-operatively.

†† *Large or small group, working in pairs.*

🕐 *45–60 minutes.*

Previous skills/knowledge needed

Although the order of the activities is not important, this activity links with 'Detective work' (page 84) and the children should experience both.

Key background information

The children need to understand how a circuit is made through experimenting with making circuits in different ways. They should appreciate that a circuit needs to be complete before electricity can pass all the way round, thus lighting the bulb. When they are experimenting, they should discover that electrical connections need to be made at the bottom and the side of the bulb in order to complete the circuit. (See Figure 1.)

It is important that they do not form misconceptions, the following being common examples among pupils of this age:

▲ A circuit needs two pieces of wire to make it work.

▲ Some coloured plastic coatings

Figure 1

on wire help to make a better circuit than others.

▲ A bulb needs a holder to make it work.

Make sure that the voltages for the bulbs and the batteries are the same. A 4.5V battery will blow a 1.5V bulb.

Language to be introduced

circuit, bulb, holder, crocodile clips, switch, battery, wire

Preparation

Collect enough equipment for each pair to have a battery and holder, a bulb and holder, three pieces of different-coloured plastic-coated wire with crocodile clips at each end, three pieces of wire without clips.

Resources needed

Batteries and holders, bulbs and holders, wires with and without crocodile clips, small screwdrivers, containers for the equipment; writing materials; one copy of photocopiable sheet 143 per pair of children.

What to do

Show the children the set of equipment. Hold up the bulb and ask the children where they have seen bulbs and what they are used for. Then explain that they are going to find out how to light up a bulb. One or two children can be given the opportunity to make the

circuit; while the others are watching this, remind the children about the names of the various electrical components.

Then give out photocopiable sheet 143 and talk to the children about investigating each type of circuit shown. Check that they are not developing misconceptions (see above). Sometimes one piece of wire will seem to work better than another as a better connection is made. Children then may think that it is the colour that is important, not the connection. Remind the children that they will need to work carefully to test each arrangement. They can then invent two different circuits of their own, draw them in the last two boxes, and test them.

Suggestion(s) for extension

The children can create more elaborate circuits, test these and record them on their own. They could use their library skills to find some written information on circuits and write it up in their notebooks.

The children could swap the bulb for a motor in the circuit, and see what effect this has.

Suggestion(s) for support

If the children are paired appropriately, they should be able to support each other. It may be necessary to talk with some children to help them clarify the idea that a complete circuit needs to be made before the bulb will light.

Assessment opportunities

From the children's discussion and their completed activity

sheets, it will be possible to assess their understanding of a circuit and what is needed to light a bulb. While they are working in pairs, an assessment can be made of their ability to work co-operatively.

Opportunities for IT

The children could use a drawing or art package to create pictures of their circuits. They will need to be shown how to draw lines (possibly of different thicknesses) and change the colours to match the colours of the wires used. However, this is not an appropriate stage to introduce circuit diagrams using conventional symbols.

Display ideas

Some of the completed activity sheets can be mounted, and displayed beside an enlarged copy of one of the children's ideas for making the bulb light up (which the teacher may have redrawn). Add labels with questions such as:
▲ *What ideas did you have for making the bulb light?*
▲ *Did any of them not work? Why not?*
▲ *How many different ways did you find?*

Components can be left by the wall display, for children to continue to try out their ideas for making circuits.

Reference to photocopiable sheet

The children need to work in pairs to complete photocopiable sheet 143. Encourage them to work methodically and to check their findings. They will need to put a tick under each picture which illustrates a bulb that will light.

A LIGHT SWITCH ◆IDEA◆

To be able to put a switch in a circuit. To be aware of the purpose of the switch and its ability to make or break the circuit.

†† *Large or small group, working in pairs.*

🕐 *30 minutes.*

Previous skills/knowledge needed
The children need to understand how to construct a circuit, as in the activity 'Making a circuit' (page 85).

Key background information
The children need to have constructed a circuit. Some may already have thought about switches if they are relating the circuit to lighting in school or in the home. By adding a switch to the circuit, the children can control whether the bulb is on or off: they can either complete or break the circuit in a single, reversible action. In science activities, they can investigate further which materials make a good switch.

Language to be introduced
switch, break, circuit, connect

Preparation
If there are insufficient switches for each pair to have one, make some more using paper clips and fasteners (see Figure 2). Make up one circuit for teacher use.

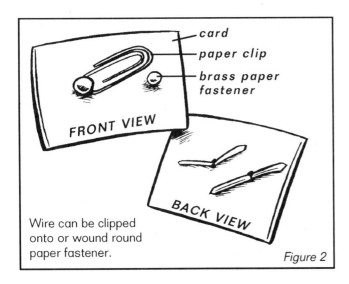

Wire can be clipped onto or wound round paper fastener.

Figure 2

Resources needed
One prepared circuit, switches, equipment to make circuits (see page 85), one copy per child of photocopiable sheet 144, scissors, solid glue sticks, blank paper.

What to do
Tell the children that they are going to make switches to turn a light bulb on and off. Talk about the light switch in the classroom, before you show the children a switch and how

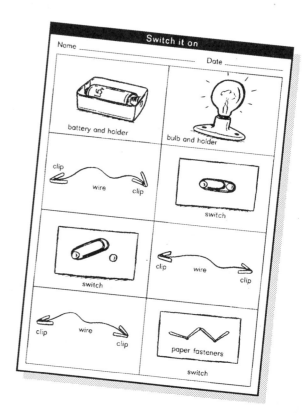

it moves on and off. Then show the children the prepared circuit and put a switch into it. Ask them to explain what they think is happening as the bulb goes on and off.

Ask the children to make a circuit, then let them experiment in their pairs to put the switch into the circuit in different places. Check with each pair that they can connect the switch and turn the bulb on and off. Ask them to explain what is happening. They may suggest that the power cannot get through when the switch is not closed.

Give out copies of photocopiable sheet 144 and discuss each of the pictures with the children. Explain that they will only need some of them to make a circuit with a switch that will light the bulb. They should cut out the ones that they need, and arrange them on a blank sheet of paper and then stick them down.

DESIGN AND TECHNOLOGY

Suggestion(s) for extension

The children can write up a report about what they have discovered, stressing the ways in which a switch's design serves its function.

Suggestion(s) for support

Individuals may need more discussion to see that there is a break in the circle (circuit) when the switch is off. When they have cut out the pictures, they may need help to arrange them into a circuit with a switch.

Assessment opportunities

Through observation and listening to their comments, it will be possible to assess the children's ability to work together and support each other, and their understanding of what a switch does in a circuit. From the photocopiable sheet, it will be possible to see which children have an understanding of how a circuit with a switch is put together (and thus of how it works).

Display ideas

The display for 'Making a circuit' (see page 85) can be extended. A switch can be added to the circuit, and a large drawing of a circuit with one of the switches in it can be put up on the wall. Add some of the finished cut-out circuit and switch sheets which the children have made.

Reference to photocopiable sheet

The children will need to cut out the shapes on photocopiable sheet 144 carefully, and fit them together to make a circuit with a switch that is on (so that the bulb will light up). Not all of the pictures will be needed.

Language to be introduced

switch, circuit

Preparation

For each pair, collect equipment to make a circuit (as in the activity 'Making a circuit' on page 85). For the switches, collect six paper clips, six brass paper fasteners, six drawing pins, three strips of tin foil, three pieces of card approx. 6cm², a piece of soft board (about 6cm²) for each pair.

Resources needed

Sets of equipment for making a switch and a circuit (see above), spare wire, paper fasteners, paper clips, masking tape, one copy of photocopiable sheet 145 per pair of children.

ON AND OFF   FPT

To be able to make an electrical switch. To develop co-operative working skills. To develop ability to follow instructions.

†† *Large or small group, working in pairs.*

🕐 *60 minutes.*

Previous skills/knowledge needed

The children need to know how to build a circuit and the effect of adding a switch to that circuit. They could gain this from 'Making a circuit' (page 85) and 'A light switch' (page 87).

Key background information

The children will be following instructions to make switches, and devising some of their own. The task will help them to work systematically and use materials for a purpose. They will also develop their cutting and joining skills.

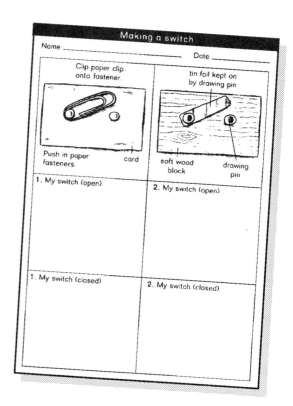

What to do

First ask the children to make a circuit, then remind them about the switch that they put into the circuit in the activity 'A light switch', and explain that, in pairs, they are now going to make some switches. They will make two switches following instructions from the photocopiable sheet, then invent some of their own. They must test each switch in the circuit to make sure that it works, then draw their switches in the empty boxes on the sheet.

Suggestion(s) for extension

The children can make and test other switches, using materials which have not already been chosen by the teacher and adapting them to fit the circuit.

Suggestion(s) for support

The photocopiable sheet can be altered so that the children are following instructions for all four switches. Some children may need additional discussion to help them make a workable switch and understand that the switch needs to be closed (completing the circuit) for the bulb to light.

Assessment opportunities

Opportunities for assessing how well the children co-operate will arise as they work in pairs. As they work with the photocopiable sheet, it will be possible to assess their ability to follow instructions; and as they make the switch, to assess their understanding of what a switch is and how it works.

Display ideas

Make a large drawing of one switch and label the parts. Mount some of the switches that the children have made together with some of the completed photocopiable sheets. Add bought switches, such as those used in the home and in models. If appropriate, put out a small screwdriver with one switch which the children can disassemble and reassemble.

Reference to photocopiable sheet

Photocopiable sheet 145 forms the framework for this activity. The children need to follow the first two diagrams, then draw in the switches which they invent in the empty boxes. Additional switches for the children to make can be drawn in the empty boxes if it is inappropriate for the children to make their own switches.

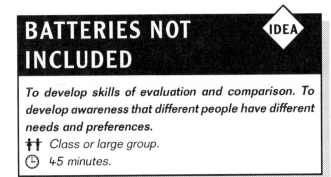

BATTERIES NOT INCLUDED · IDEA

To develop skills of evaluation and comparison. To develop awareness that different people have different needs and preferences.

†† *Class or large group.*

🕐 *45 minutes.*

Key background information

It is important that the children be aware that there is no simple answer to *Which is better?* in a case like this. People have different preferences and needs and the children should be aware of this. The value of objects can change if they no longer work as they were intended to.

Language to be introduced

battery, value, powered, preference

Preparation

Collect two similar items, one of which is battery-operated. It is important to choose two products with the same function. A toy car or a game might be appropriate.

Resources needed

Two similar objects, one of which is battery-operated (see above).

What to do

Show the items to the children and discuss what they are used for. Ask questions about their appearance and feel. What colour are they? What are they made from? Ask questions about how they were made. Were they made by hand or in a factory? How were they fixed together? Ask questions about their design. Are the items decorated attractively? Do the children like the way they look? Are they good toys (or whatever the chosen objects are)? Do the children think other people will like them?

Ask the children what will happen when the battery runs down. Will that toy be as much fun or as useful without a battery? What would happen if the owner did not have enough money to buy batteries? Encourage the children to see that people should consider this when buying a toy. Ask questions about what the objects are worth. What would they be worth

DESIGN AND TECHNOLOGY

to the children? Encourage them to answer not in terms of an amount of money, but in general terms such as 'Very valuable, it would be my best toy' or 'Not very valuable, I wouldn't really want one.'

Suggestion(s) for extension

Using the questions that were suggested in the activity as starting points and working individually or in pairs, the children could create their own 'consumer report' on one of the toys or on an object of their own choosing.

Suggestion(s) for support

Use only the battery-operated toy for the discussion and focus on an evaluation of the toy, getting the child to think about its features, construction, function and design.

Assessment opportunities

From listening to the children, it will be possible to identify children who can successfully evaluate products made by others. Listen for answers such as 'The wheels are not fixed very well to the body. It won't last long,' or 'It is solid and made from wood. It won't break easily.'

Opportunities for IT

The children could write their consumer reports on the toys using a word processor. They might be able to add a simple picture, drawn using an art package or scanned from their own line drawing or from the manufacturer's packaging (or

other literature). The reports could be printed out to form a class 'Consumer Report Book', or mounted alongside the toys to create an informative display.

Display ideas

Create a display of pairs of objects, one of which is battery-operated, which have similar functions. Possible examples include toys, games, clocks and bells. Put up questions that were used in the discussion alongside the display.

BE CAREFUL! ◇ FPT

To be aware of the dangers of playing with electricity. To make something with a mechanism. To work together co-operatively.

†† *Small groups (with adult supervision).*

🕐 *90 minutes.*

Previous skills/knowledge needed

The children need the knowledge and understanding of slides and hinges gained from the activity 'Moving on up' (page 32). From their work in science, they will need to have discussed the dangers of electricity and of playing with it.

Key background information

The children's previous work on mechanisms can be combined with the knowledge and understanding that they have gained through a science activity on the dangers of electricity, in order to produce a safety poster warning others of the dangers of playing with electricity. The children need to made fully aware, in this activity, of the dangers of not acting in a safe way. They will also need to be reminded about mechanisms and how they make things move in different directions. As this is an FPT, there are many constraints on them, including the size of the finished product and the type of card which they will use.

Language to be introduced

dangers, mechanism, slide, electricity, hinge

Preparation

If possible, find a picture which illustrates the dangers of playing with electricity. Make hinge and slide mechanisms (see page 32) to show the children. Collect scrap card, such as old cereal boxes (open the boxes out). Cut up some best card into 40cm squares.

Resources needed

A picture to illustrate the dangers of playing with electricity, examples of hinges and slides, scrap card, best card cut into 40cm squares, scissors, Pritt sticks (one between three or four children), brass paper fasteners, a large piece of card on which to mount the finished pictures, drawing materials.

What to do

If there is an appropriate picture available, use it in a brief discussion to remind the children about the dangers of electricity. Explain that they are going to make a poster to be displayed to remind them and other children about the dangers of playing with electricity. They will each make one picture, and then these will all be fitted together to make up the poster. To make it more convincing, they will use a mechanism in their picture.

First, discuss with the children the things to avoid if they are near electricity. These might include: climbing on pylons, playing with kites near pylons, touching plugs and sockets, playing with electrical items near water, pulling at electrical leads and pushing things into sockets. If they are not sensible, then they may electrocute themselves and die.

Make sure that each child in the group has one idea to contribute to a poster. Remind the children about the slide and the hinge which they used in 'Moving on up' and show them some examples. Help the children to decide which mechanism they will use to show movement in their picture. For instance, they might use a slide to show a child climbing a pylon or a kite flying near wires. Allow them time to design and make a model of the final picture in order to try out their mechanism. They may want to draw the design, but modelling it in scrap card is sufficient. Talk with them about any problems which they encounter, and help them to suggest solutions. When they are satisfied with their model, let them make the final product. Remind them constantly about achieving a quality finish by cutting neatly and colouring in the picture carefully.

Suggestion(s) for extension

The children can make up a questionnaire to find out if other pupils are aware of the dangers of electricity. These could be given out to one or more classes before the display of the posters around the school, and given out again afterwards to see if there have been any changes in the children's awareness.

Suggestion(s) for support

Some children may need to be given an idea as a focus for their picture, and be shown how to make a mechanism before they can make one themselves.

Assessment opportunities

Through observation of how the children work, discussion and evaluation of the finished product, it will be possible to assess which children have an understanding of the dangers of playing with electricity and of how a slide or a hinge mechanism works. From their finished products, the children's ability to produce a quality product can be assessed.

Opportunities for IT

The children could use a word processor to create labels for their posters. They would need to think about type size and the suitability of different fonts, and the size and colour of the lettering.

Display ideas

The finished posters can be displayed around the school. Their effect could be evaluated (see 'Extension ideas').

A BRIGHT-NOSED MONSTER

To develop children's skill in making circuits with switches. To extend their ability to follow instructions and work co-operatively.

†† *Small group, working in pairs.*

🕑 *90 minutes.*

Previous skills/knowledge needed

The children will need to have knowledge of how to make a circuit and a switch, which could be gained through the activities 'Making a circuit' (page 85) and 'On and off' (page 87).

Key background information

This activity focuses on applying the knowledge and skills which the children have acquired in previous activities so that they can incorporate a circuit and a switch into a product.

Language to be introduced

circuit, bulb, wire, crocodile clips, switch, battery, holder

Preparation

Provide enough smallish boxes and equipment to make circuits and switches for each pair of children. Small cereal boxes, cake boxes or tea boxes are ideal. Turn the boxes inside-out and seal them up with masking tape. The children then have plain card surfaces to decorate. Make up sets of equipment for each pair to include a battery and holder, a bulb and holder, two pieces of wire each about 15cm in length (crocodile clips optional), two paper clips, two brass paper fasteners and two small pieces of card (approx. 6cm square). If you prefer to leave the ends of the wires bare, the wires can be attached to the battery holder and switch using masking tape; otherwise, use crocodile clips. Make copies of photocopiable sheet 146 and put each pair of sheets into a plastic sleeve for protection.

Resources needed

Boxes (approx. 15–20cm in length and width), prepared sets of equipment (see above), masking tape, spare scraps of card, scissors, felt-tipped pens/crayons for each table (about three pairs of children to a table), copies of photocopiable sheet 146 in plastic sleeves (one set per pair of children).

What to do

Tell the children that they are going to make a monster whose nose lights up. Quickly remind them about how to make a circuit and a switch, using one of the sets of equipment prepared. Give out the photocopiable sheets and discuss each step with the children. Discuss the importance of a step-by-step approach, the need to do things in the correct order and the possible consequences if they do not.

First, the children should make a circuit and check that it works. Then they should make a switch and try it in the circuit. It is important that they check whether the bulb lights before they try to attach the circuit and switch to a model. Next, they can cut away the box so that the back is open, and make the nose by cutting a small hole with scissors for the bulb to go through. Discuss what will happen if they make a hole that is much larger than the bulb.

Next, the children will need to fix their circuit and switch into the box and

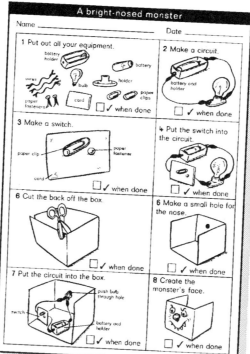

check that they are still working. Finally, they can create the monster's face around the nose by drawing and colouring it carefully.

Suggestion(s) for extension

The children can put in one or two glowing eyes, using another circuit.

Suggestion(s) for support

Appropriate pairing can be used to provide support for those who may need it. Instead of using a switch, the children can just take the crocodile clip off one end of the battery holder to make the bulb light up and go out.

Assessment opportunities

From observing the children, it will be possible to see those who can work together co-operatively, persevere and achieve a quality product. Although the children are working in pairs, it may be possible to assess an individual child's understanding of a circuit and a switch through questioning and observation.

Opportunities for IT

The children could use an art package to create the monster's face, either before the activity (so that the model fits the face) or once the model has been made (so that the face fits the model). The printed face can then be cut out and glued onto the box.

Display ideas

The monsters' faces will make an exciting display. The instruction sheets can be enlarged and displayed alongside the models to show how they were created.

Reference to photocopiable sheet

The children will have photocopiable sheet 146 at the beginning of the activity, and the teacher will discuss the sequence of instructions with the children. The sheet should be accessible throughout the activity; the children should be encouraged to refer to it constantly, working through the sequence of instructions in a step-by-step manner.

DESIGN AND TECHNOLOGY

Mouldable materials

This chapter contains IDEAs and FPTs relating to the use of mouldable materials in construction. Through working with these materials, children will have the opportunity to design and make products, and to acquire knowledge and understanding of these products and their purpose, people's needs and preferences, safety and appropriate vocabulary. The designing skills developed include discussion of ideas, modelling of ideas, exploration and investigation of mouldable materials, finishing, use of colour, shape and texture and evaluation by the children of their own ideas. The making skills developed include cutting, combining, moulding and shaping, joining, finishing and evaluating their own products. The knowledge and understanding gained covers the investigation, disassembly and evaluation of a variety of mouldable materials, how mouldable materials can be used and how well the products fit their purpose, the need for safe handling of tools, how to work safely and the importance of using the correct vocabulary.

The following contexts are particularly appropriate for work with mouldable materials: festivals and celebrations, homes, containers, animals, minibeasts and ourselves.

⚠ Non-fungicidal pastes should be used (fungicidal pastes can cause skin irritation), and children should be well covered when working with mouldable materials. No reference is made to firing clay in kilns, as many schools do not have access to one. If there is access to a kiln, it can be used; relevant safety precautions should be taken.

DESIGN AND TECHNOLOGY

DRYING OUT ◆ IDEA

To develop the children's investigative skills.

†† *Class or large group.*

🕐 *Session 1: 20–30 minutes. Leave for about a week.*
Session 2: 20–30 minutes.

Previous skills/knowledge needed

Some understanding of evaporation would be useful. The children should relate this activity to any previous work on change in materials.

Key background information

Materials can change. When some materials are left in the open air or heated, they loose their moisture and become brittle.

Language to be introduced

mouldable, investigation, surface, brittle, change, smooth, crumble, sticky

Preparation

You will need some clay that has been stored properly. Cover a table with plastic sheeting (if none is available, use paper) and provide enough aprons for the children. Make a chart on which to record the children's ideas.

Resources needed

Clay, aprons, newspaper, one copy per child of photocopiable sheet 147.

What to do

Session 1

Sit the children so that they can all see the clay, and ask them to roll up their sleeves. Talk about how the clay is stored. Show them a piece of clay that has been stored in moist conditions. Ask them to describe what they see, write their ideas on a chart. Ask the children to feel a small piece of the clay. Ask for words that will describe how it feels. Encourage them to use correct vocabulary such as *soft, mouldable, smooth, sticky, wet, moist.*

Now ask them for their ideas about how to find out what would happen to the clay if it dried out. They may suggest putting some in the sun or on the radiator. Set up an investigation, making sure that the children think about carrying out a fair test. (If different groups of children do this activity, they could put the clay to dry in different places.) They would need to think about having some clay that is kept moist, using the same amount of clay and leaving it for the same length of time. Ask the children to write up their investigation using photocopiable sheet 147. Leave a notebook by the clay, so the children can record their observations each day. Leave the clay for about a week.

Session 2

Look at the clay with the children. Ask them about the similarities and differences they can see between this clay and the way it was before. Encourage them to look for changes in colour and texture (particularly in terms of mouldability), and to use appropriate vocabulary such as *brittle, breaks easily, hard* and *crumble.* Ask the children to write their conclusions in the final section on their photocopiable sheet.

Suggestion(s) for extension

The children could investigate further the changes that occur when clay is dried out. For example, they could weigh the clay before and after it dries out to see if the weight changes; and they could add water to the dried clay to see if it returns to its original state.

Suggestion(s) for support

The children may need support filling in their investigation sheet. If it is appropriate, one sheet could be filled in by the whole group, using one or two scribes.

Investigating clay

Name _____
Date _____
What we want to find out:

What we need:

What we did:

What we found out:

DESIGN AND TECHNOLOGY

for certain purposes and not others. Different people like, and have different uses for, different products.

Language to be introduced
This will depend on the collection of items that is made. Possible words include: mouldable, hard, shape, flexible, bendy, change.

Preparation
Make a collection of items (four to six) that have been made from mouldable materials such as wire, papier mâché, clay, Mod-Roc, play dough, modelling clay, plastic. Try to include some items from a range of cultures.

Resources needed
A collection of items (see above), one copy per child of photocopiable sheet 148.

What to do
Put out the collection of objects so that the children can see them. Discuss with the children:
▲ what each object is;
▲ what it is used for;
▲ what it is made from;
▲ other objects that are made from the same material;
▲ why the object is made from that material;
▲ whether it could be made with a different material (and if not, why not);
▲ who would use it;
▲ whether they would like one and why/why not;
▲ what they do not like about it.

Assessment opportunities
From the children's comments, it will be possible to assess their ability to describe and understand some of the characteristics of a material. From their writing on the photocopiable sheet, it will be possible to assess their ability to record observations and their understanding of the investigation process.

Display ideas
Display some moist clay, wrapped up in clear polythene to keep it moist, and some dried-out clay, together with some of the investigation sheets mounted on card.

Reference to photocopiable sheet
Photocopiable sheet 147 provides a framework for the children to use in writing up their investigation. They will need to fill in the first three sections when they have set up their investigation, and the last section when the investigation is completed.

USEFUL THINGS

To develop the children's evaluative skills.
†† *Class or large group.*
🕒 *45 minutes.*

Previous skills/knowledge needed
Allow the children time, before the activity or at the start of the activity, to explore the items. Links should be made between this activity and others where the children have used their knowledge and skills to evaluate products.

Key background information
Because of their properties, mouldable materials are used

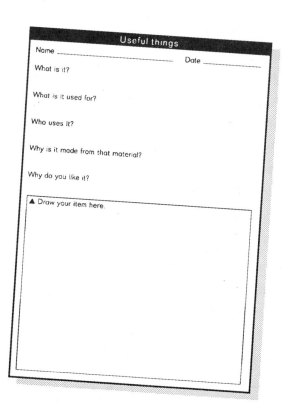

Useful things
Name _____ Date _____
What is it?
What is it used for?
Who uses it?
Why is it made from that material?
Why do you like it?
▲ Draw your item here.

DESIGN AND TECHNOLOGY

Encourage them to listen to each others' views and ideas. It is important for them to understand that other people may like something that they do not. If there are objects from other cultures which have the same purpose as, but a different appearance to, something with which the children are familiar, such as a Japanese teacup or ornament, encourage the children to understand that these items are not necessarily better or worse than the familiar ones. Ask the children to choose the item which they found most interesting and to fill in photocopiable sheet 148.

Suggestion(s) for extension

The children could evaluate a wider range of useful objects or different designs of the same objects, such as a cup.

Suggestions for support

Take out or refocus those questions which are not appropriate for the children.

You may have to scribe for some children who need help to fill in their photocopiable sheet.

Draw into the discussion children who need extra encouragement to speak.

Assessment opportunities

From the discussion and their work on the photocopiable sheet, it will be possible to assess the children's ability to evaluate. From their drawings and labels, it will be possible to assess their observational skills and ability to communicate their ideas.

Opportunities for IT

The children could use an art or drawing program to draw one of the objects, or a part of it (for example, the pattern used for the decoration).

Display ideas

Display the range of objects, together with some of the questions that were asked in the discussion. The objects could be grouped in various ways: material, making process, function, appeal and so on. Add some of the completed photocopiable sheets.

Put up pictures of various objects and display the questions alongside these.

Reference to photocopiable sheet

The children should fill in the chart on photocopiable page 148 about the nature of the object and its use, then complete an observational drawing of their chosen object.

TORN APART   ◆IDEA

To develop the children's skills of disassembly and investigation.

†† *Large or small group.*

🕓 *45 minutes.*

Key background information

Papier mâché is made from layers of torn-up paper. It has certain properties which change when the material dries out.

Language to be introduced

papier mâché, dried out, moist, brittle, paste, wet, crack, magnifying glass

Preparation

Prepare some small bowls of water-based paste and add small pieces of torn paper to make papier mâché. Make this

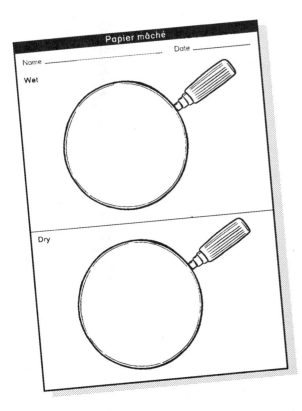

Papier mâché

Name _____ Date _____

Wet

Dry

▲ what it feels like;

▲ what it smells like;

▲ what it sounds like when squeezed in the hand.

Put up their ideas on a chart. Now let the children pull first the wet and then the dry papier mâché apart very carefully. Encourage them to see that the wet pulp is mouldable and bendy, but the dry pulp is stiff, brittle and inflexible.

Ask them to look at both the wet and dry papier mâché samples with a magnifying glass. Discuss their observations with them. Encourage them to look for the layers and to see if these look the same on the wet as on the dry pulp. Explain that they are going to fill in photocopiable sheet 149 to show what they have found out (by drawing what they see through the magnifying glass, and writing labels beside the drawings). Encourage them to keep referring back to the papier mâché samples as they fill in the sheet.

Suggestion(s) for extension

The children could investigate further the properties of the dried-out papier mâché to find out, for example, if it is waterproof or if it is brittle.

Suggestion(s) for support

Some children may need help to use a magnifying glass and to complete the photocopiable sheet.

a few days before the task, so it has time to dry; make some more papier mâché during the task. Provide magnifying glasses (one per child).

Resources needed

Wet and dry papier mâché; paste brushes, one magnifying glass per child, one copy per child of photocopiable sheet 149.

What to do

Encourage the children to work in pairs and examine first the dried-out, then the wet papier mâché. Ask them to describe:

▲ what it looks like;

Assessment opportunities

From the discussion and their work on the photocopiable sheet, it will be possible to assess the children's skills of observation and their understanding of the role that moisture plays in a mouldable material.

Display ideas

Display some dried-out papier mâché, together with some of the completed photocopiable sheets. Papier mâché objects (dried but not finished) could be displayed to show the

DESIGN AND
TECHNOLOGY

properties of the dried-out pulp. A papier mâché model sawn in half provides a dramatic image of the structure of this material.

Reference to photocopiable sheet

The children should fill in their observations of both the wet and the dry papier mâché by drawing and writing on photocopiable sheet 149. Keep reminding them to look at the papier mâché through the magnifying glass, and draw what they see carefully. They can make detailed drawings and label them from different viewpoints, such as the side (layers, edges) and underneath (shape, feathered/smooth outline).

WHEN I KNEAD YOU   ◆ IDEA

To develop the children's investigative and disassembly skills.

†† *Large or small group (to sit around a table).*

🕐 *30 minutes.*

⚠ *Make sure the children are aware of relevant hygiene procedures to be followed before and after handling salt dough. The dough must **not** be eaten.*

Previous skills/knowledge needed

The children will need to draw on their knowledge about the correct storage of mouldable materials, and how materials can be disassembled and reassembled.

Making dough

flour		2 cups
salt		1 cup
water		1 cup

1. Put the flour and the salt into a bowl.

2. Slowly add some water and combine with a knife.

3. Keep adding water and combining until the dough will just stick together, but is not wet.

Figure 1

Key background information

By assembling and combining the right ingredients, it is possible to make dough. Some mouldable materials need to be stored in airtight containers and away from heat for them to remain mouldable.

Language to be introduced

dough, salt, measure, knife, ingredients, sieve, flour, water, bowl, combine, mouldable, cup

Preparation

Make a small quantity of salt dough to show the children. Collect the ingredients, aprons and tools needed. Make a recipe card (see Figure 1, which could be enlarged on a photocopier or used as a basis for your own card) and put it in a plastic sleeve.

Resources needed

Flour, salt, a cup, a knife, a bowl, aprons (one per child), a recipe card (see Figure 1) in a plastic sleeve.

What to do

Sit the children around a table and show them the salt dough. Break off pieces, so that all the children can feel a piece of it. Ask them if they know or can guess how it is made. Encourage them to talk about the ingredients and the process of making the dough. If they have already made bread or pastry, links could be drawn with these activities. Record their ideas on a chart.

Now show them the ingredients that are needed to make salt dough. Let them feel the flour and sieve it. Add the salt and then gradually add the water. Start to show them how to combine the ingredients with the knife, then let each have a turn. If they have combined other ingredients when working with food, discuss the different ways of doing this. Talk about the changes as they are happening, and make comparisons with the finished dough. If the dough is sticky, ask the children what they could do to make it 'drier' and then add a little more flour. If it will not hold together, discuss the need to add a little more water to help the ingredients bind together.

When the dough is made, review with the children the ingredients that they started with, the changes that occurred and what the end product is like. Explain that you are going to store the dough until they have time to use it. Discuss with them why it is important to keep it in an airtight container, away from heat. If the children have experience of storing clay, make links with this.

Suggestion(s) for extension
The children can make their own salt dough, following the recipe in Figure 1. They could suggest ways of trying to disassemble the dough in order to get back the original ingredients. They could then plan and carry out investigations to see whether their ideas work. Subsequent discussion of their results will be needed, to establish the idea that some changes are not wholly reversible.

Suggestion(s) for support
Discuss the process of making dough with individual children who may need help to understand the changes that are taking place.

Assessment opportunities
Take note of those children who understood that dough is a single material made from a number of different ingredients.

MAKE AND BAKE

To develop the children's skills of making, including shaping and finishing.

†† *Large group.*

⏲ *Session 1: 30 minutes. Session 2: 30–45 minutes.*

Previous skills/knowledge needed
The children could have the experience of making dough in the 'When I knead you' activity (page 98) before this task. If not, they should complete the activity after this task.

Key background information
It is possible to mould moist dough into any shape. When the dough is dried out, it is hard and its shape cannot be changed (except by breaking it). When dried, it can be finished or decorated in a variety of ways.

Language to be introduced
mould, dough, bake, shape, heat, hard

Preparation
Prepare some salt dough and store it appropriately. (A suitable recipe is shown on page 98.) Cover the tables with plastic sheeting (or newspaper) and put out small boards for the children to work on. For Session 2, prepare appropriate paints and provide thin paintbrushes.

Resources needed
Salt dough, plastic sheeting (or newspaper), small boards, paint, thin paintbrushes, a plastic knife, drawing materials, an oven.

What to do
Session 1
Open the storage container which contains the salt dough. Give each child a small piece and ask them to mould it in their hands. Talk about how it feels, using vocabulary such as *mouldable, soft, smooth*. (Refer back to making the dough, if the children have already done this.) Explore the dough by asking the children to roll it into a ball, to roll it flat, to break it or cut it with a knife, and to put it back together. Ask different children to suggest a shape that all the children could make. Ask the children if there are any shapes that they think cannot be made, then try making these.

Now ask the children to make something with the dough. They could be:

▲ given a free choice;

▲ asked to make something which links with the class topic;

▲ asked to make something which links with a story they have recently heard.

Put the models in the oven for 30 minutes at 150°C. Leave to cool.

Session 2

Either at the end of the previous session or before this one, the children can draw the item that they have made and design the decoration (using paint) that they will add. Talk with the children about their choice of colours. Before they decorate their models, talk about how the material has changed. Include discussion of the fact that it is not mouldable now and cannot change its shape. Then let them finish their products. When they are finished, help the children to evaluate their work. Questions to ask might include:

▲ *Is it fit for its purpose?*

▲ *Is it what it is supposed to be?*

▲ *Are the colours appropriate?*

▲ *Are you pleased with the appearance?*

▲ *Would you make any changes next time?*

Suggestion(s) for extension

The children could make a similar product using Plasticine, and note any differences between the two finished products. They may note that the Plasticine model is not hard, and that it is not possible to paint its surface.

Suggestion(s) for support

Individual children may need further discussion to extend their vocabulary. Some children may need help to mould their dough into a suitable shape. Some may need further discussion about the concept of change and how heating has affected the dough.

Assessment opportunities

From the children's comments, it will be possible to assess their knowledge of this mouldable material and their understanding that heat can change the material so that it is no longer mouldable. Their ability to design an appropriate decoration for their item can also be assessed.

Display ideas

Display the finished products around a large recipe card for the dough and the individual ingredients used to make the dough. (You may wish to enlarge the recipe shown on page 98; or the children could prepare their own.) Baked, finished products could be displayed alongside similar objects in earlier stages of preparation, to give a sense of the making process as one involving several steps.

A THUMB POT   ◇ FPT

To develop the children's making skills, particularly in shaping and finishing. To develop the children's design skills, particularly relating to pattern and the use of colour.

✝✝ *Session 1: large group. Session 2: small groups.*

🕒 *Session 1: 30 minutes. Session 2: 30 minutes.*

Previous skills/knowledge needed

The children should have previous knowledge of what happens to clay when it is dried, possibly from the activity 'Drying out' (page 94).

Key background information

Moist clay can be moulded and smoothed to a chosen shape. When dry, it can be painted.

Language to be introduced

clay, mould, pot, thumb

Preparation

Check that the clay is mouldable. Cover the tables with plastic sheets (or newspaper) and provide an apron for each child. For Session 2, provide mixing palettes, thin paintbrushes and a range of paint colours for each group.

Resources needed

Aprons (one per child), clay, paints, thin paintbrushes, mixing palettes, a small pot of water for each group.

What to do

Session 1

Make sure that the children are wearing aprons and that their sleeves are rolled up. Give each child a piece of clay. Give them time to investigate the material. Suggest that they mould it, roll it, squeeze it. Ask them to describe what it can do and what it feels like. If they have carried out the 'Make and bake' activity with salt dough, encourage the children to make links between the two materials by asking them about similarities and differences.

Now explain that they are going to make a thumb pot. Get them to make a ball of clay by rolling it around in their hands. The ball should be smooth; they may need to add a tiny amount of water with one finger over the surface to smooth away cracks. They can then put the clay on the table and push their thumb carefully into the middle of the ball. Explain that what they have just made is called a 'thumb pot'. They may need to push the clay up gently around their thumb with their other hand. They should check the surface of the clay, both inside and outside the pot, to make sure that it is smooth. Leave it to dry.

Session 2

Either at the end of the previous session or at the start of this one, ask the children to draw a design for the decoration on their pot. They could look at other pots or pictures of designs, to gain ideas. Then they can transfer the design onto their pot, using paint.

When the pots are finished, evaluate them with the children. Ask such questions as:
▲ Is it fit for its purpose?
▲ Is it actually a thumb pot?
▲ Is it smooth on the outside and the inside?
▲ Are you pleased with its appearance?
▲ Is the finish good (the paints have not run and the colours and pattern are attractive)?
▲ Would you make changes next time?

The children can then draw and/or paint a picture of one of the finished pots (not necessarily their own).

Suggestion(s) for extension

The children can use different-shaped or different-textured items to press and print into the surface of the clay. Let them try out items and designs on spare pieces of clay before working on their pots. Let the children research the use of mouldable materials in a range of cultures: clay is used for a variety of household goods, and for personal decoration such as jewellery.

Suggestion(s) for support

Some children may need help to mould the pot around their thumb and to paint a pattern onto the pot. Talk with children individually to encourage them to give a detailed evaluation of their finished work.

Assessment opportunities

From observing the children, it will be possible to assess their ability to shape and finish a product. From their design drawings, it will be possible to assess their ability to produce an appropriate design and to select from a range of colours. From discussion, it will be possible to assess the children's ability to evaluate their own products and suggest changes to them.

Opportunities for IT

The children could use an art package to design the pattern for their thumb pot before transferring it onto the pot itself.

Display ideas

Make a display of commercial and/or handcrafted objects that have been made from clay. Add questions to the display to encourage the children to look at how the objects have been made and what decoration has been added.

Make a display of the children's pots and put up some of the drawings of them. Add the question 'Can you match the drawing with the pot?'

DESIGN AND TECHNOLOGY

BENT OUT OF SHAPE ◀FPT▶

To develop the children's understanding that wire can be bent into many shapes, then returned almost to its original shape.

†† *Class or large group.*

🕐 *30 minutes.*

⚠ *If wire is used for this activity, make sure that the ends are taped over.*

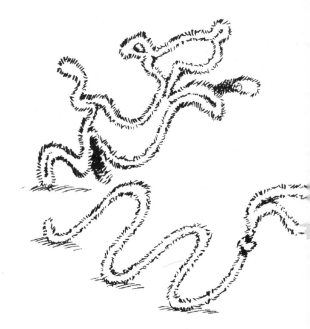

Previous skills/knowledge needed

The children can draw on knowledge and practical and evaluative skills that they have gained from other activities with mouldable materials.

Key background information

Wire can be bent into a variety of shapes, because it is a highly flexible material. Unlike, say, string, it will keep its shape against gravity. A bent piece of wire can be returned almost to its original shape (the point at which it was bent is likely to remain kinked). Wires can be joined by twisting them around each other.

Language to be introduced

bend, flexible, join, wire

Preparation

Decide how many pipe cleaners the children should use and what they should make. Provide enough pipe cleaners for this purpose. Cut some of the pipe cleaners in half, so that each child can have a small piece to investigate. Cut a length of wire and make sure that the ends are taped over.

Resources needed

Pipe cleaners, a length of wire (coat-hanger wire is appropriate).

What to do

Show the children a piece of wire, and find out what they already know about wire. Ask the children if they can think of some everyday objects that are made from wire. Show them some examples, using pictures from catalogues and/ or real objects. Discuss the reasons for the use of wire in preference to other materials: it is flexible; it is light; it does not break easily; and it can be made into many different shapes.

Give out the small pieces of pipe cleaner. Allow the children time to investigate this material. Show them that there is wire underneath the textile covering of the pipe cleaner, and ask them to feel the wire along the length of the piece. Encourage them to bend and shape it, and to return it to its original shape.

Ask the children to work in pairs, joining their two pieces of wire. Review what they have found out. Discuss the facts that the wire will not snap, that it can be joined by twisting and that it can make any shape. Then suggest that the children make something with their pipe cleaners. They could:

▲ have a free choice;

▲ make something that is linked to their topic;

▲ make an animal;

▲ make a container.

Ask the children to draw the pipe cleaner object that they like best from those made in the class, and to write down their reasons for this choice. Encourage them to expand on 'Because it is nice'.

Suggestion(s) for extension

The children could add decoration to their models, using the shape as a framework which they can then cover with materials such as card, fabric or papier mâché. Use this as an opportunity to discuss construction frameworks, such as scaffolding.

Suggestion(s) for support

The children may need help to bend and join the pipe cleaners. An adult may need to talk with the children individually about their choice of a favourite model and the reasons for their choice.

Assessment opportunities

Make a note of which children use appropriate vocabulary to describe how the wire can be moulded and its shape changed.

Opportunities for IT

The children could use an art or drawing package to plan what they intend to make or record what they have made. The line drawing features of this type of software link well to the use of pipe cleaners. The children will need to know how to draw straight and curved lines and change the thickness

of the line. They may also wish to change the colours or extend their single diagram into a more elaborate picture.

The completed pictures could be printed out and bound to make a class book of models. A picture might also be added to a word processing package, so that the children could add the reasons why they liked a particular model.

An alternative way of displaying this work might be to create a multi-media presentation using an authoring package. A title page could present the names of the modellers or a rough sketch of the model itself. When the child clicks on the model on the title page, he or she is taken to the information about the model – which might include the name of the child who made it, information about how it was made and what others thought about it, and the drawing created using the graphics program. Children could even add spoken text, recorded using a microphone attached to the computer.

Display ideas

Display the finished models, the children's drawings of their favourite model and the reasons for their choice. Add labels to show the purposes of the various models.

HARD PAPER FPT

To develop the children's designing, making and evaluative skills.

†† *Group.*

🕐 *Session 1: 30–45 minutes. Session 2: 20–30 minutes. Session 3: 30 minutes.*

⚠ *Check that the paste is not a fungicidal one. Make sure that the children wash their hands after they tear newspaper and wear aprons while working with the papier mâché.*

Previous skills/knowledge needed

The children will need to draw on the knowledge and understanding of papier mâché which they acquired in the 'Torn apart' activity (page 96). They will also draw on their design skills and their ability to make choices.

Key background information

The fact that when paper is soaked with paste and water it is pliable and tears easily, and when it is then allowed to dry it becomes hard and inflexible, is the same for whatever method of making papier mâché is used.

Language to be introduced

papier mâché, wet, pliable, stiff, paste, dry, hard

Preparation

Get the children to tear some newspaper and coloured tissue paper into small pieces and keep these in separate containers. This can be an ongoing activity over a number of days (or even weeks). Mix the paste just before the task, cover the tables, and provide enough aprons and plastic tubs for each child. For Session 3, provide different-coloured paints, mixing palettes and thin paintbrushes.

Resources needed

Plastic sheets (or newspaper), coloured tissue paper, two large plastic containers, Vaseline, paste, brushes, aprons, plastic tubs, paints, thin paintbrushes, mixing palettes, pencils, blank paper (for drawing and painting).

What to do
Session 1

Explain to the children that they are going to make some papier mâché. Give them the small plastic tubs which they will use, and ask them to grease the outside all over with Vaseline. While they are doing this, ask them why they think they are using the grease. Write down their suggestions on a chart, which they can refer to later. Then show them how to paste the torn pieces of newspaper and put them on the tub. Talk about the need to have an even coverage, so that the thickness of the finished container is the same all over. Show them how to put a layer of plain paper or coloured newsprint between each layer of white newsprint, to help them check that they have covered everywhere before adding another layer. While the children are working, make a container using a non-greased tub (or get one of the children who is working quickly to do this). When the children have put on several layers (five to seven), let them decide whether they want to finish off the container with a layer of tissue paper. Leave the pots to dry for two or three days.

Session 2

Before the pots are to be painted, give out paper and pencils. Ask the children to decide what their container will be used for and how they will decorate it. For example, if it is for a friend, what colours and shapes does he or she like? Remind the children that their pots are small, and that it will be difficult to do very big patterns on them. Ask them to draw, and then paint in, a design on their sheet of paper. It is important that they design the pattern before applying it. They should consider (for example) the pattern's colour, size and shape, and how it will be applied, so that they have a clear understanding of how the design fits onto the pot. The purpose of the pot may be a relevant factor here.

Session 3
Put out the materials and equipment that the children have chosen (when designing) to use. Ask all the children to slip off their papier mâché containers from their tubs. Stress how important it is to do this slowly and carefully; encourage the children to work in pairs if appropriate. Show the children the container that was made over the ungreased tub. Ask them what they think will happen when you try and take it off. It should be difficult to do this: the children should understand that the grease is used to stop the paper sticking to the tub. Encourage the children to reproduce the designs they have already drawn and painted when they paint their containers. The finished containers should be left to dry. The children could add a varnish to their products afterwards.

Suggestion(s) for extension
Children could use books and CD-ROMs to research the use of papier mâché today, in times past and in other cultures.

Suggestion(s) for support
Children could work in pairs to cover a tub. Individuals may need help in transferring their designs to their pots.

Assessment opportunities
From watching how the children work, it will be possible to assess their ability to work independently, to make a product in stages and to use a design to add a quality finish.

Opportunities for IT
The children could design a pattern for the whole exterior of their container, using an art or drawing package. They could start by drawing the outline of the shape that would be made if the papier mâché could be peeled from the pot in a single piece (like orange peel). This would give them a rectangular or trapezoidal shape, depending on the shape of the pot.

Display ideas
Display the finished pots together with the children's design drawings/paintings. Use the pots in the display to hold objects such as pencils, dried flowers (not in water) or beads.

DESIGN AND TECHNOLOGY

Design and make assignments

Design and make assignments must give children the opportunity to show their capability in relation to the National Curriculum level descriptions. A wide range of designing and making skills will already have been developed and practised in the IDEAs and FPTs that the children have undertaken; but the design and make assignments (DMAs) in this chapter will give the children opportunities to make choices about the materials, techniques and finishes that they use, and will help them to identify a need or purpose for their product within the context provided by the teacher. When discussions take place with the children at each stage of the assignment, it is vital that they are encouraged to select, choose and decide for themselves from a range of options. If these opportunities are not given, then the children will be unable to show that they can operate at higher levels of design and technology capability.

However, in order to make the assignment manageable in the classroom, there have to be a structure and certain constraints. In the 'real world', designers and manufacturers have constraints such as time, cost and limited availability of materials placed on them, and it is important that the children understand this. For each assignment, therefore, the constraints can be adapted to suit the materials, time and facilities which are available.

Photocopiable sheet 157 is a general evaluation sheet, which could be used for any DMA in this chapter.

DESIGN AND TECHNOLOGY

DMA LESSON PLANS

Since the design and make assignments are to be used for assessing the level at which the children are working, the format in which they appear differs slightly from that of the other activities:

▲ A list of 'Typical resources needed' is given for each assignment, as the precise choice of resources will depend on the children's judgement.

▲ The following guidelines on support, assessment and opportunities for IT are applicable to all of the assignments.

Suggestions for support

During an assignment, if a child needs individual support then it should be given by a peer or adult. There is little point in leaving the child to become frustrated and give up on the task. However, the support should be noted, and the amount of support given will be reflected in the final judgement about the level at which the child is operating. Discussion and an examination of the materials available at the planning stage may help to prevent the children from attempting tasks which are too difficult for them.

Assessment opportunities

The assignments give you the opportunity to assess the children's designing skills (their ability to think up ideas, to do research, to sketch their ideas, to try things out, to plan their work and to evaluate their designs) and their making skills (their ability to work accurately with a range of materials and tools, to plan their projects and to evaluate their finished

products). When the children have completed an assignment, you can use the verbal, written and practical evidence you have collected to decide which of the level descriptions for Attainment Target 1 (Designing) and Attainment Target 2 (Making) best describes the work of that child. This is recorded as the level of design and technology capability at which they are working. Remember that this is a 'best fit' approach. It should not be necessary to retain all the assessment evidence for all the children in the class: just keep what you think is appropriate to provide a range of evidence for one assignment, indicating the levels reached.

It will be more appropriate for the school to compile a portfolio of children's work, containing drawings, photographs of practical work and evaluations of typical work at each level. It should include the work of children from different classes and different academic years, and should be reviewed as new work is added and older work is removed. This portfolio will provide an essential moderation document within the school, and will give new members of staff an indication of the kind of work that is appropriate at each level.

Opportunities for IT

In this chapter, the 'Opportunities for IT' sections have been altered to provide teachers with a number of possible activities, linked to the design and make activity, that would enable assessment of some aspects of IT capability to be made. Clearly, it would be impossible for every child to undertake every activity suggested for each DMA; but over a period of time, the teacher might wish to select a single activity that would give the child an opportunity to show his or her level of IT capability (as judged against the level descriptions) in one aspect of information technology.

The teacher could suggest activities or direct the child to a particular activity; for example, over the year each child might write, edit and print out one evaluation of a DMA, or use a graphics program within the design process. Of course, there will be similar opportunities from other areas of the curriculum which could be used alongside the suggested activities.

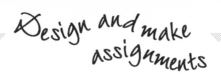
SHELTER FROM THE STORM

To design and make a shelter for a purpose. To make a stable structure.

†† *Working individually and in pairs.*

🕐 *Three one-hour sessions.*

⚠ *Make sure that the children use saws and bench hooks in an appropriate (safe) manner.*

Previous skills/knowledge needed

The children should have an understanding of stability and of strong and rigid shapes, and have had experience of using a range of construction materials and techniques (including a variety of methods of joining materials). They should have had opportunities to experience the main aspects of designing and making. Links can be made with the activities in chapters on Structures, Reclaimed materials and Construction kits. Terms that have been introduced should include *construction kit* and *stability*.

Key background information

The children will have the opportunity to make a shelter for a particular person or animal. Therefore it is important that the children are clear about the requirements for the shelter when they are designing it. They will need to think about its size, its shape, the materials from which it will be made, and perhaps the need for it to withstand wind and rain. The completed shelter can be evaluated against these original criteria.

Preparation

If you are sharing construction kits with another class, check that the kits will be available when you need them. Decide on the context for the assignment. You might ask the children to decide who they will make their shelter for, or to make a shelter which links to a class topic (such as homes, animals or farms) or to a story about a lost animal looking for a home.

Typical resources needed

Square sections of wood, bench hooks, junior hacksaws, clamps, garden canes, art straws, twigs, moss, soil, construction kits, string, masking tape, wool, Plasticine, fabric, brass paper fasteners, ribbon, pipe cleaners, one copy per child of photocopiable sheet 150.

What to do

Tell the children that they are going to make a shelter. After they have looked at the materials available, discuss with them the types of shelter that they could make. Draw their ideas on a chart, so that they do not forget all the possibilities; add some yourself if appropriate. They may suggest tents, brick or stone shelters, or ones made from natural materials. Discuss what materials they might use for their model shelters, and show them the range of materials available. (If appropriate, they could collect others that they have suggested.)

Ask the children to decide who (or what) they are going to make their shelter for. The next stage is for them to decide what kind of shelter they will build and what materials they will use to do it. Ask them to work in pairs, talking about these two decisions. Impose a time limit, say two minutes. Then give out copies of photocopiable sheet 150 and ask each child to put her or his ideas down on paper. Encourage them to explore the materials to help them with their ideas.

When they are ready to make the shelters, remind them to work safely and carefully. During the making, remind them about their original criteria for their individual shelters (written on the activity sheet). When they have finished, help them to look back at their original criteria and to see whether they have met them.

Suggestion(s) for extension

The children can test whether their shelters are waterproof (using a sprayer) or wind-resistant (using a battery-operated fan).

Opportunities for IT

The children might display their IT capability by using a:

▲ graphics program to draw a picture of their shelter, either before or after they have made it;

▲ word processor to write a description about how they

DESIGN AND TECHNOLOGY

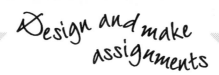
made the shelter, or why they designed it in the way they did;

▲ word processor to write, edit and print an evaluation of their shelter for display alongside the model they have made.

Display ideas
The shelters can be displayed together with models of the people or animals that they are intended for.

Reference to photocopiable sheet
Photocopiable sheet 150 needs to be given to the children when they have some clear ideas about the shelter they will make. Remind them that they can draw several ideas on the back of the sheet before making their final decision.

THE VILLAGE BUS

To design and make a village bus which will not get stuck on a muddy road. To demonstrate the ability to select appropriate wheels for a model vehicle. To demonstrate the ability to attach wheels so that they can turn.

†† *Working individually.*

🕑 *Four one-hour sessions.*

⚠ *Make sure that the children use saws and bench hooks appropriately. Supervise the use of the glue gun. Remind the children of the dangers associated with electricity (if they are doing the extension activity).*

Previous skills/knowledge needed
The children should have gained knowledge and understanding of different types of wheels, and how wheels are fitted to a chassis, from previous IDEAs. They should have had experience of using a range of construction materials and techniques (including a variety of methods of joining materials), and have had opportunities to cover most aspects of designing and making during FPTs. Links can be made with activities in the 'Reclaimed materials', 'Mechanisms' and 'Construction kits' chapters.

Terms that have been introduced should include *axle, axle holder, chassis, bus, pneumatics, balloons, syringe* and *tubing*.

Key background information
The story given in photocopiable sheet 151 is adapted from a popular African children's story. A fuller version is given in *Our Village Bus* by Maria Mabetoa Mzwakhe (published by Raven Press, South Africa, 1985).

The children should be familiar with putting wheels on vehicles; but here, the focus is on choosing the type of wheels which will be appropriate to allow the bus to move through mud without sticking. In addition, the children can be encouraged to think of other design features – such as a

scoop on the front to pick up mud – which may help to stop the bus sticking. (They may be able to incorporate a pneumatic system into their bus to work a mechanism of this kind.)

Preparation
Put some copies of photocopiable sheet 151 in the library corner, for the children to read in their own time. Provide appropriate materials from which the children can make wheels. Find a large tray and fill it with mud.

Typical resources needed
Construction kits, boxes of different shapes and sizes, brass paper fasteners, card wheels, wooden wheels, cotton reels, dowel, straws, a hole punch, masking tape, Blu-Tack, scissors, PVA glue and spreaders, a glue gun (to be used under supervision), treasury tags, string, cylindrical tubes, a small amount of corrugated card, cellophane, tissue paper, felt-tipped pens, paints and brushes, Plasticine, tubing, syringes, balloons, a cutter for tubing, square sections of wood, junior hacksaws, bench hooks, clamps, several copies of photocopiable sheet 151. (Bulbs and holders, batteries and holders, wire, switches for the extension activity.)

What to do
Read the 'Village Bus' story (see photocopiable sheet 151) to the children, and spend some time discussing the part where the bus got stuck. Ask the children to explain why it could not move. Tell them that they are going to make a bus for the village, and ask them to think about how they will

make it so that it is able to go through the mud without sticking. Do the wheels need to be smooth, or do they need to grip the surface in order to push the bus forward? The children may suggest special wheels or scoops for the mud. Write or draw their ideas on a large chart, so that everyone can see.

Now ask the children to plan making a bus for the village. Allow individual children to share their ideas with the others. You may want to suggest certain things that they should think about – such as shape, getting into the bus and the type of wheels that they will use – and identify the criteria that they need to be aware of when they make their bus. Show the children the materials that they can choose from, but remind them that they can ask for other things if they need them. You may want to remind them about different cutting and joining techniques which they could use. The children should draw their designs and/or try out different wheels which they might use (modelling). Ask the children to explain their design drawing to a friend, and to check whether there are any obvious problems which they have missed.

Before they move on to make their buses, encourage the children to collect all the items that they need and to think about the order in which they will assemble the pieces. As they are making their models, remind the children about the need for a quality finish. Ask the questions: *Do your wheels turn round?* and *Will they be able to pass through the mud?* Provide a large container of mud in which the children can check their wheels.

When the buses are finished, go back to the original criteria and ask the children to evaluate their products against these. Identify which (if any) criteria have not been met, and discuss how they might change their buses so that all the criteria are met.

Suggestion(s) for extension
The children could make people to go in the bus. This would

require them to consider the size and weight of the passengers as criteria when designing and making the vehicle.

The children could add lights to their buses, using circuits and switches.

Opportunities for IT
The children might display their IT capability by using a:
▲ graphics program to create labels to put on the side of the bus;
▲ word processor to write and edit their version of the story;
▲ word processor to write, edit and print an evaluation of their bus, to be displayed alongside the model they have made.

Display ideas
Ask the children to paint a background scene of the village and display their finished vehicles in front of it, together with a copy of the story. Add a question: *Which wheels do you think will help the bus to move through the mud?*

Reference to photocopiable sheet
The children can read the 'Village Bus' story for themselves using photocopiable sheet 151; but initially it is meant for the teacher, to enable him/her to set the context for the activity.

IN THE BAG

To design and make a bag for a particular purpose. To choose appropriate finishing techniques for the bag.
†† *Working individually.*
🕒 *Four one-hour sessions.*

Previous skills/knowledge needed
The children should have studied a range of bags, and explored a variety of ways of joining, in IDEAs. In FPTs, they should have learnt how to use a pattern, how to join pieces of fabric and how to add decoration to the fabric. (Make sure that the children understand the use of the word *pattern* in this context.) They should be familiar with the main aspects of designing and making.

Key background information
The children should already have looked at a variety of bags; but they will need to focus on the purpose of, and the particular features needed for, a bag of the kind described here. It will be important for the number of items put in the bag to be limited, as the pigs (se below) could not carry much and the children may not be able to make a large bag anyway. Two key features of the evaluation will be to see whether the items fit in the bag and whether the bag is strong enough to hold them; other criteria, such as the bag's appearance, will be less important.

DESIGN AND TECHNOLOGY

Preparation

Provide a version of the story of the Three Little Pigs (if possible, one which has pictures of them with their bags). Set up a display of bags – such as carrier bags, shopping bags, rucksacks and shoulder bags – a few days before starting the assignment, so that the children have had the opportunity to examine them.

Typical resources needed

To make bag: a selection of fabrics and plastics, a stapler, needles, sewing threads, embroidery threads, fabric paints (for printing), paintbrushes, thin paper (to make a pattern), plastic-headed pins, fabric, ordinary scissors, pinking shears, Velcro, fabric glue, very large press studs, elastic, large buttons, ribbon. To keep in bag: a toothbrush, toothpaste, nighwear, a cuddly toy, biscuits, a book, a key, a pencil, a notepad.

What to do

Read the children the story of the Three Little Pigs. Discuss with them the need for each pig to have a small bag in which to put his overnight things when leaving home. Remind the children that the items need to be small, like those for a doll (an adult's pyjamas would not fit a piglet), and that the bag cannot contain too much or it will be too heavy for the pig to carry. Decide together what would go in the bag; select items from the collection that you have provided, and leave them for the children to see. Put out a range of fabrics, joiners and finishers that the children may wish to use. It may be possible for the children to collect their own items for the bag if the assignment is carried out in separate parts.

Discuss with the children what kind of bag they are going to make and what needs to go in it. Ask them what they need to think about. This may include the size and type of bag, the materials they will use to make it and the way in which they will finish it. When you and the children have identified the criteria for the bag, the children can draw their designs. Encourage them to talk to each other about their designs and the reasons for the decisions they are making. You can focus questions on parts of the children's designs

that are not clear, or that you think will not work.

As the children are making their bags, remind them about neat cutting and joining to produce a quality finish. When the bags are completed, the children can test them to see whether they will hold the overnight items for the pig. Then they can look at the other criteria that were decided on, and judge whether their bags meet these.

Suggestion(s) for extension

Children could think of additional criteria to meet, such as that the bag must be waterproof and should be carried on the pig's back.

Children could design and make secure fastenings for the bags, and research the different kinds of locks on suitcases.

Opportunities for IT

The children might display their IT capability by using a:
▲ graphics program to draw a picture showing the design of the bag;
▲ graphics program to design a pattern for the bag;
▲ word processor to write, edit and print an evaluation of their bag, to be displayed alongside the model they have made.

Display ideas

A display of the bags can be made, together with the story book and the possessions that the pigs are going to take away. A collage or painting of the three pigs can be made as a background to the display.

SWEET DELIGHT

To design and make sweets for a particular purpose. To choose appropriate shapes, colours and flavours for the sweets.
†† *Individual and small-group or paired work.*
🕐 *Four one-hour sessions.*
⚠ *Make sure that strict hygiene rules are followed during the making and storing of the sweets.*

Previous skills/knowledge needed

Through IDEAs, the children should have gained knowledge about the importance of food's appearance and the fact that different people have different tastes. Through FPTs, the children should have gained skills in mixing, combining, shaping, assembling, finishing and evaluating and have a range of designing and making skills. Links can be made with the 'Food' chapter.

Key background information

The key choices that the children will make relate to shape, flavour and colour. They should think of the person for whom they are making the sweets, and make choices based on what they think that person would like. It may be more appropriate for you to decide on the purpose for the sweets, such as a school sale – in which case, the children would need to consider what they think the visitors to the sale might prefer. The children could work in pairs. If they do so, there will be opportunities to assess their ability to co-operate with each other. Remember that the sweets should be kept for a limited time (not longer than 24 hours) in the fridge before they are eaten.

Preparation

Provide enough icing sugar (200 grams per child). Check that you have enough equipment for the children to use, including a range of flavourings and colourings and a disinfectant spray. Put copies of the recipe sheet (photocopiable page 153) in plastic covers for protection. Make up a small amount (about 75 grams) of the icing sugar mix just before the start of the activity.

Typical resources needed

A selection of sweets, icing sugar, mixing bowls, metal forks, small containers for water, dessert spoons, scales and/or cup measures, different flavourings and colourings, straws, rolling pins, different-shaped small cutters, paper plates, doilies, cling film, plastic covers for tables, cloths to wipe tables, a disinfectant spray, washing-up facilities, hand towels, one copy per child of photocopiable sheet 152, one copy per pair/small group of photocopiable sheet 153.

What to do

Display a small selection of sweets so that the children can see them. Talk with the children about the ways that different sweets are produced for different purposes. Chocolates can be a special gift, boiled sweets can be sucked if you have a sore throat and shaped sweets can be made for a particular occasion. Tell the children that they are each going to make some sweets (probably seven or eight) from an icing sugar mix, and that they have to decide who the sweets will be for and what they will look like.

Show the children a bowl with a small amount of the icing sugar mix made up, and the selection of cutters, food colours and flavourings which they can use. Ask them what they will need to think about when they are designing their sweets – this may include colour, shape, size and flavour. Allow the children time to make their decisions and then share these with the whole group. Then the children can record their designs and plans on photocopiable sheet 152.

Before the children start to make their sweets, remind them about the hygiene rules – in particular, to tie back long hair, take off rings, put on aprons and wash hands. As the children start to make their sweets, using recipe sheet 153, remind them not to add the water too quickly: just a dessertspoonful at a time. They may need help to add the

colouring and flavouring. Using a straw should help with this (see illustration below).

When they have made their sweets, they can arrange them on their plates with a doily, keeping two sweets back for tasting (if strict hygiene rules have been kept). The sweets

Lift thumb to release straw.

for tasting can be cut into pieces. Children should taste each other's sweets and say which they like best. The original criteria need to be looked at, and the children should decide whether these have been met. Their comments can be recorded on the activity sheet. The sweets can then be covered in cling film to give to the person for whom they were made. The children can bring back comments from the receivers of the gifts at a later time.

Suggestion(s) for extension

The children can make their own templates for sweets and cut round them. They could select a ready-made box or make up one from a net and decorate it for their sweets.

The children could research the making of sweets by a local sweet manufacturer. They could find out about the different processes involved and the health and hygiene rules observed.

Opportunities for IT

The children might display their IT capability by using a:

▲ word processor to write and print a list of four important hygiene instructions, to be displayed in the classroom (they will need to use a large font);

▲ graphing program to display the results of the class tasting, indicating which sweets looked or tasted the best;

▲ word processor to write, edit and print an evaluation of the sweets that they have made.

Display ideas

Photographs could be taken of the plates of sweets. These could be displayed together with a recipe sheet (or card) and some of the children's design drawings and evaluation comments.

Reference to photocopiable sheets

The children will need to fill in photocopiable sheet 152 when they have thought out their designs, and when they have evaluated the sweets. Photocopiable sheet 153 can be copied onto card, put into a plastic cover and put on the table so that each child can see a copy while making the sweets. Check that the children are able to follow the instructions.

WEATHER CHART

To design and make a chart for representing weather. To choose appropriate mechanisms for moving parts on the chart.

†† *Working individually.*

🕐 *Four one-hour sessions.*

Previous skills/knowledge needed

From IDEAs, the children should have experience of investigating a range of mechanisms. From FPTs, they should have gained skills in cutting and joining card and paper and in making a variety of mechanisms; they should also have gained knowledge and understanding about how these mechanisms work. Links can be made with the 'Mechanisms' and 'Reclaimed materials' chapters. Terms that have been introduced should include *mechanism, hinge, wheel* and *slide*.

Key background information

The key focus of this activity is on the children's knowledge of mechanisms and their ability to select an appropriate one for their chart. In addition, the children need to be aware of different types of weather and how these can be represented pictorially.

Preparation

Cut out, from newspapers and magazines, some examples of ways of representing different types of weather. Mount these, so that the children can use them for ideas. Provide examples of the mechanisms that were involved in 'Moving on up' in the 'Mechanisms' chapter.

Typical resources needed

Reclaimed card (for example, from boxes), sheets of card in different colours, tissue paper, crêpe paper, coloured paper, sticky paper, solid glue sticks, PVA glue and spreaders, masking tape, brass paper fasteners, treasury tags, paper clips, scissors, a stapler, a hole punch, coloured pencils and crayons, felt-tipped pens, Blu-Tack, A3 paper (for charts).

What to do

Talk with the children about different types of charts – such as colour, birthday and number charts – that are in the classroom or the school. (It may be necessary to take a short walk to look more closely at some of these.) Ask the children to work in groups, deciding what features are needed to make a good chart. They may suggest clear lettering, bright colours, large pictures, a title. Write these ideas up as a reminder.

Now talk to the children about the need for a weather chart, to show what the weather is each day. Ask them what they will need to consider when they make their chart – in particular, the mechanisms they will use how these will show the different types of weather. Discuss with them the need

DESIGN AND TECHNOLOGY

LIVING DOLL

To design and make a jointed puppet. To choose how to finish the puppet.

†† *Working individually.*

⏱ *Four one-hour sessions.*

⚠ *Make sure that the children use saws and bench hooks appropriately. Supervise the use of the glue gun.*

to show one day's weather at a time. (The chart is a changeable display, rather than a permanent record.) It may be that they need to be able to move a pointer, or cover some of the pictures on the chart. Remind them about the mechanisms which they have made in the past, and bring out examples which were made in the activity 'Moving on up' (see page 32). Then they can begin to sketch out the chart with the mechanism(s) which they intend to use.

When they have a clear idea of the intended product, they should make a model of it with reclaimed card. They can then make any necessary changes before using best card to make their final product. Remind them about cutting neatly, and drawing and colouring clear pictures, to produce a quality finish.

When the charts are all completed, put them up in the classroom so that the children can use them every day. Evaluation can take place after the children have had a good opportunity to assess how effective their charts are.

Suggestion(s) for extension
Some children could make a large chart for the front entrance hall or another class. They could use their evaluation of their own charts to produce a new chart, which includes the modifications they have suggested.

Opportunities for IT
The children might display their IT capability by using a:
▲ graphics program to draw pictures for use on their weather chart;
▲ word processor to write labels for use on their chart;
▲ word processor to write, edit and print an evaluation of their chart, to be displayed alongside the finished chart.

Display ideas
The charts could be displayed, along with mounted examples of ways of representing different types of weather pictorially.

Previous skills/knowledge needed
The children should ideally have investigated a range of puppets and come to an understanding about how they are assembled. Through the FPTs in this book, they should have had experience of measuring, cutting, joining and assembling with construction kits, card, reclaimed materials and wood. They should also have experienced a range of finishing techniques with paints, paper and fabrics. Terms that have been introduced should include *puppet* and *joint*.

Key background information
This activity will give the children the opportunity to choose the type of puppet that they want to make and select an appropriate mechanism (or combination of mechanism) to allow it to move. They will need to consider the puppet's size, as well as the finish that they will give to it. They should be encouraged to cut and join carefully, and to design the finish before they start to add hair and clothing. This will help to ensure that they make a quality product.

Preparation
A few days before you start the activity with the children, put out a collection of puppets for them to look at, together with examples of the different ways of joining materials explored in the activity 'Making a hinge' (page 42).

Typical resources needed
Card, boxes, cylindrical tubes, egg boxes, brass paper fasteners, lollipop sticks, a heavy-duty hole punch (for the lollipop sticks), string, elastic, wool, treasury tags, scissors, a normal hole punch (for paper), masking tape, cotton wool, fabrics, PVA glue and spreaders, fabric glue, coloured pencils and crayons, one copy per child of photocopiable sheet 154.

What to do
If the children do not have experience of puppets, show them the range of puppets that have been on display. Talk with them about how these are put together and how they move. Discuss with the children the reason for making the puppet in this assignment. It may be that the children need a puppet to perform a play or retell a story, or that there are no puppets to go with a new puppet theatre in the class. Once the children have a purpose for the puppet, they can decide what character they would like to make. The next stage is to ask the children how they will construct the puppet so that it can

DESIGN AND TECHNOLOGY

move. Ask them about the ways that they know of making something that can move. Ask them what parts of the puppet could move. Now remind them about different ways of joining that they have tried, and show them examples from the activity 'Making a hinge' (page 42).

When the children have looked at the materials available to them, they can sketch out their design for the puppet on photocopiable sheet 154. They need to indicate how it will be jointed so that it can move, what materials they will use to make it and what the finished puppet will look like.

Suggestion(s) for extension

Where appropriate, encourage children to give their puppets a more complex range of movements. They could put in more joints, add strings and work the puppet with them, or add a stick to the body so that they can move it from a distance.

They could investigate the mechanisms of different kinds of puppet, including ones seen on television.

Opportunities for IT

The children might display their IT capability by using a:
▲ graphics program to create a design for their puppet;
▲ word processor to write, edit and print an evaluation of their puppet.

Display ideas

The finished puppets can be displayed. If they have been made for a play, background scenery could be built and/or painted and the puppets displayed against it, together with a copy of the play. Bought puppets can be added to the display to show that there are many kinds of puppet.

Reference to photocopiable sheet

The children will need to fill in all three parts of photocopiable sheet 154. Check that they know what has to go in each section (drawing in the first and third sections, writing in the second section).

PRESENT TIME

To design and make a gift from clay for a particular person.

†† *Working individually.*

🕐 *Three one-hour sessions.*

Previous skills/knowledge needed

The children should have gained knowledge about clay from IDEAs, and skills in working with clay from FPTs. They should have covered the main aspects of designing and making. Terms that have been introduced include *mould, shape, coil, slab, thumb pot, plaque,* and *rolling pin.*

Key background information

It is important that the children are given time to consider what gift they can make for their chosen person. Once the context has been set, the children can be given a few days to consider what they will make. They could make a pot, a vase for dried flowers, a wall plaque or a model animal. They will have the opportunity to roll, mould and shape the clay using appropriate tools, and to decide on a finish which might include imprinting, painting and/or varnishing.

Preparation

Check that the clay has not dried out, and that you have varnish available. Collect a variety of things which could be used for imprinting, such as metal and plastic bottle caps, pen caps and plastic straws.

Typical resources needed

Clay, boards, rolling pins, items for imprinting, a plastic knife (for cutting clay), varnish, paint, brushes, clay tools, one copy per child of photocopiable sheet 155.

pushed into salt dough. The children could make a range of gifts to sell at a school sale.

Opportunities for IT
The children might display their IT capability by using a:
▲ graphics program to design and print out a gift tag to go along with their gift;
▲ word processor to write instructions on how to make a similar gift;
▲ word processor to write, edit and print an evaluation of their gift.

Display ideas
The children could display their gifts – or, if these have been given away, their finished photocopiable sheets could be displayed – with a label such as 'Do you like the gifts we have made?'

Reference to photocopiable sheet
The children should not be given photocopiable sheet 155 until they have decided what they are going to make and have decided on a final design. Stress that they can draw several ideas, and that they do not have to make just one design. They can use another sheet of paper, or the back of their activity sheet, for this.

What to do
First, show the children the clay which they can use to make the gift. Remind them how to use clay for modelling. Get them to brainstorm, in groups, what they could make as a gift, and then to share their ideas with all the class. Then discuss who the children will make their gifts for. It may be related to a special occasion (such as a birthday), or it may be just because the person is a friend. Having decided upon the recipient, the next stage will be to decide what gift that person would like. The children could think about the person's tastes, interests and favourite colours.

When they have decided what to make, the children can fill in photocopiable sheet 155. Their sketch of the gift should indicate what materials they will use and what finish they will add. As the children make their gifts, remind them about giving the product a quality finish. They will need time for the clay to dry before they can add the finish.

For evaluation, it may be possible to collect comments from the people who have received the gifts. Obviously, this will need to be handled sensitively; but it would be useful to get positive comments which highlight criteria that the children had thought of. Finally, the children can add their own 'second thoughts' about how they might amend their ideas the next time.

Suggestion(s) for extension
The children could choose from a wider range of mouldable materials, such as papier mâché, salt dough or wire, when making their gift. They could combine different materials – for instance, papier mâché on a wire frame or glass beads

---

ROOM FOR EVERYONE

To design and make a room.
†† *Working in pairs.*
🕑 *Five one-hour sessions.*
⚠ *Make sure that the children use saws and bench hooks appropriately. Supervise the use of the glue gun. Remind the children of the dangers of playing with electricity.*

Previous skills/knowledge needed
Through FPTs, the children should have gained knowledge, understanding and skills relating to sawing wood, measuring, cutting and joining with a variety of materials. In addition, they may draw on their knowledge and understanding of electric circuits and switches and their ability to incorporate these into a model. Terms that have been introduced should include *structure*, *stable*, *quality finish*, and *join*.

Key background information
In this activity, the children are given the opportunity to work with a partner while still making individual items. They may have to compromise, and to make choices between available designs, materials and colours. They should be able to use a wide range of cutting and joining skills with a variety of materials. Size will be an important consideration: however good the room is, it will be useless if the people do not fit in.

DESIGN AND TECHNOLOGY

Preparation

Provide a doll's house or a collection of pictures of play houses, for the children to use as a source of ideas. Collect some appropriate-sized play people, or make them out of pipe cleaners.

Typical resources needed

A doll's house (or pictures of play houses), play people, a collection of shoe boxes (or similar), strips of wood or offcuts, bench hooks, junior hacksaws, clamps, scissors, fabric, sponge, PVA glue and spreaders, glue gun (to be used under supervision), snips (for teacher use), masking tape, stapler, hole punch, brass paper fasteners, treasury tags, scraps of different kinds of paper, sheets of white paper, paints and brushes, old wallpaper books, a collection of reclaimed materials, needles and thread, fabric paints, bulbs and holders, batteries and holders, wire and cutters, one copy per pair of photocopiable sheet 156.

What to do

Show the children some play people, and discuss the need for the people to have rooms to live in. Working in pairs, the children can decide which room they would like to make for the people and brainstorm what should go in it. When they have finished, they could exchange ideas with other pairs who are making the same kind of room. Show the children the boxes and other materials available for making the rooms, so they can start to think about how much will fit into the room, what materials they will use and what size the fixtures and fittings need to be.

In pairs, they can then start to plan on paper (using photocopiable sheet 156), deciding exactly what they will make, what from and how. The children may need to be reminded about the walls and the floor. You could encourage the children to decide who does what, if they do not think of dividing the work. As they make the room, remind the children to follow their plan (if possible) and to make things that have a quality finish. When the rooms are completed, the children can put the play people in them and show the rooms in use. Evaluation might include questions about appropriate size, the colour scheme, the suitability of the furniture for a particular room and the quality of the finish.

Suggestion(s) for extension

The children may be able to put several rooms together to make a house (or flat). It may be necessary to make an extra room to complete the house. The children could add electric circuits for lighting.

Opportunities for IT

The children might display their IT capability by using a:
▲ graphics program to design and print a patterned wallpaper for their room;
▲ word processor to write, edit and print an evaluation of the their room.

Display ideas

The rooms can be displayed together with the children's design sheets. Toys or model people (or animals) could be put in the rooms, and shown using the furniture or other amenities.

Reference to photocopiable sheet

Filling in photocopiable sheet 156 will help to focus the children's attention on what they need to consider when designing the fixtures and fittings for their room. It may be that both children in a given pair will fill the sheet in, or that one will act as a scribe. Encourage the children to annotate their drawings.

Photocopiables

The pages in this section can be photocopied for use in the classroom or school which has purchased this book, and do not need to be declared in any return in respect of any photocopying licence.

They comprise a varied selection of both pupil and teacher resources, including pupil worksheets, resource material and record sheets to be completed by the teacher or children. Most of the photocopiable pages are related to individual activities in the book; the name of the activity is indicated at the top of the sheet, together with a page reference indicating where the lesson plan for that activity can be found.

Individual pages are discussed in detail within each lesson plan, accompanied by ideas for adaptation where appropriate – of course, each sheet can be adapted to suit your own needs and those of your class. Sheets can also be coloured, laminated, mounted on to card, enlarged and so on where appropriate.

Pupil worksheets and record sheets have spaces provided for children's names and for noting the date on which each sheet was used. This means that, if so required, they can be included easily within any pupil assessment portfolio.

Photocopiable sheets 150 to 157 can be used for the purposes of summative assessment and accompany the activities in the 'Design and make assignments' chapter.

DESIGN AND
TECHNOLOGY

Tower of strength, see page 14

Tower of strength

Name _____   Date _____

▲ Build the tower.	What happened to the tower?
	What happened to the tower?
▲ Build a tall, stable tower. Draw it.	My tower is stable because

DESIGN AND TECHNOLOGY

Let's stick together, see page 15

Let's stick together

Name _____   Date _____

▲ Build the two walls.

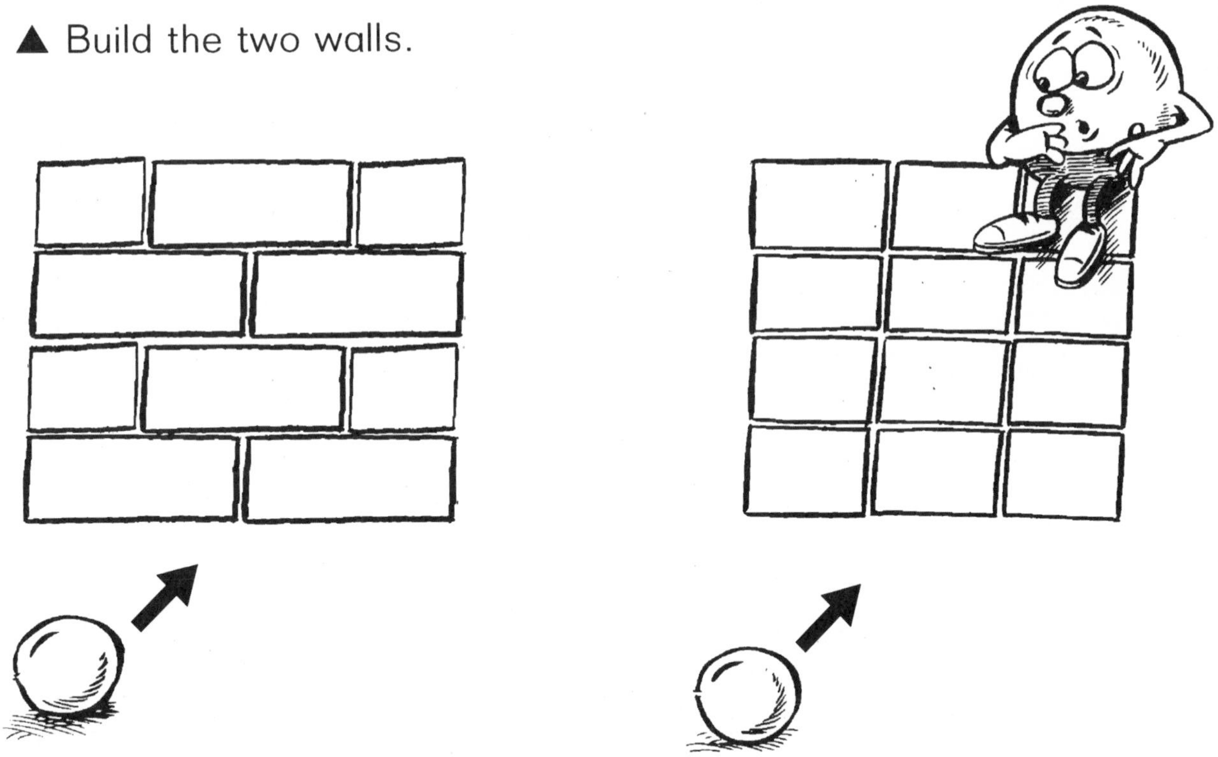

▲ Roll the ball.
What happens?

Which wall is the more stable?
▲ Draw it here.

DESIGN AND
TECHNOLOGY

Standing still, see page 16

Standing still

▲ Cut out the shapes.
▲ Cut along the dotted lines.

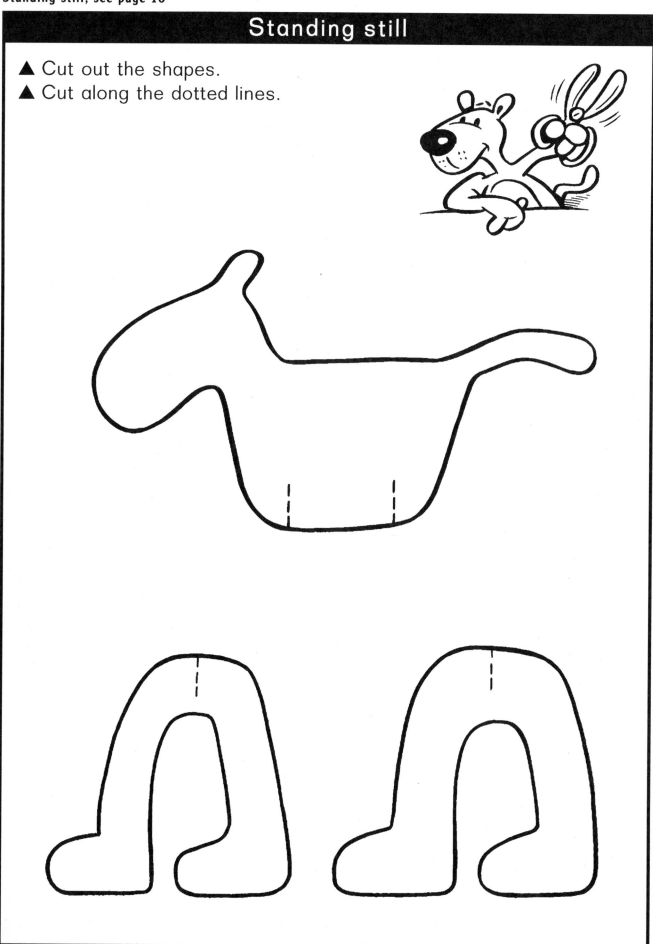

DESIGN AND TECHNOLOGY

Is the table stable?

Name _____   Date _____

▲ Draw the legs on the tables.

DESIGN AND
TECHNOLOGY

In the frame, see page 19

In the frame

Name _____ Date _____

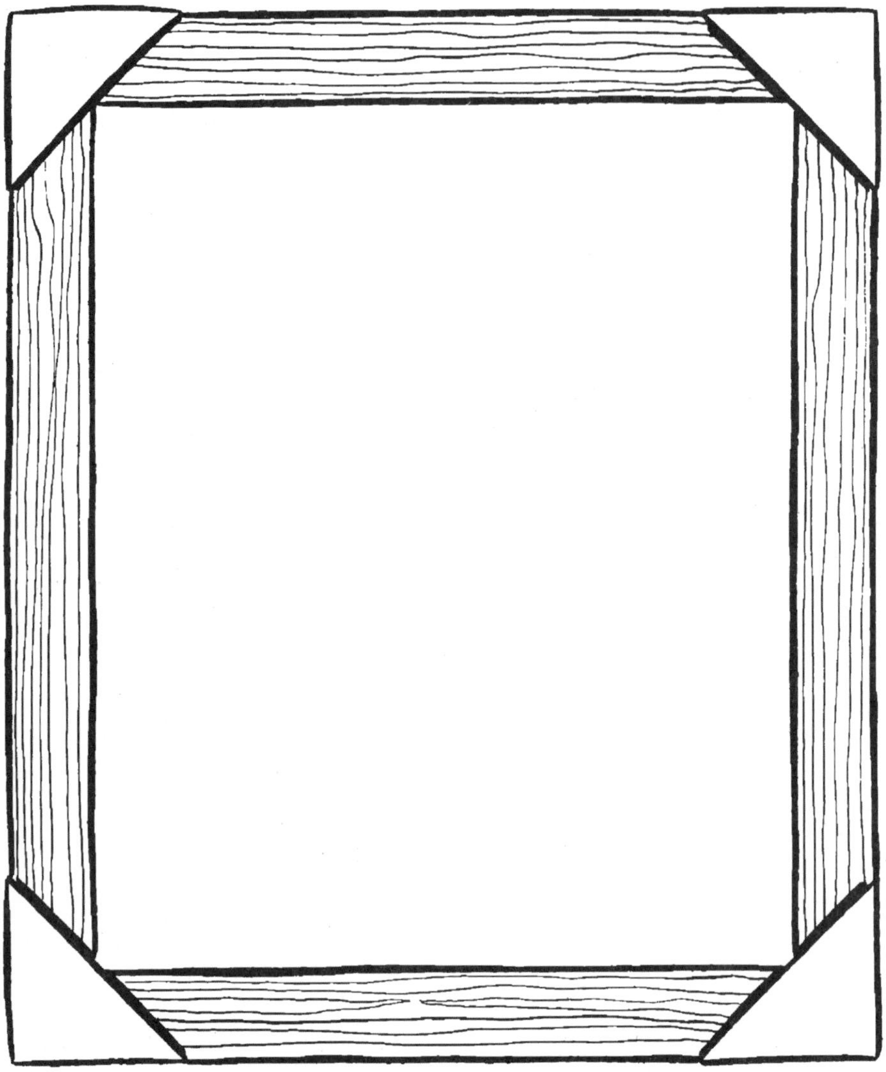

How well did you do?
▲ Tick the right face.

I put the triangles on neatly.

I used a small amount of glue.

I cut the wood accurately.

My frame is rigid.

DESIGN AND TECHNOLOGY

Sawing wood, see page 21

Sawing wood

Name _____ Date _____

Design for my furniture

It is a _____ It is for _____

How well did you make it?

I made a _____ for _____

It was stable.

It was comfortable.

I joined it neatly.

I worked safely.

I worked well with my partner.

DESIGN AND TECHNOLOGY

Which mechanism? see page 28

Which mechanism?

Name _____   Date _____

▲ Show which of the sets of three mechanisms is right for cards A, B and C, by writing the correct letter in each mechanism box.

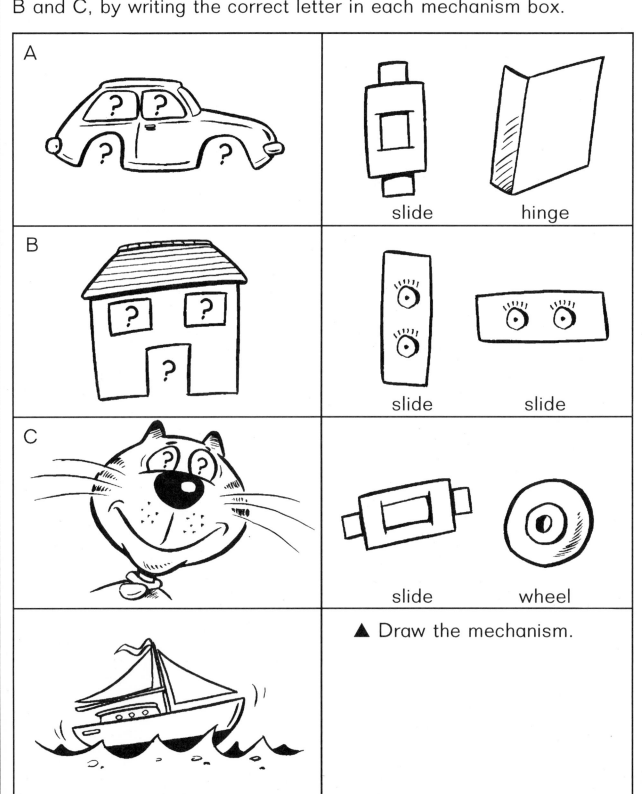

A

slide   hinge

B

slide   slide

C

slide   wheel

▲ Draw the mechanism.

DESIGN AND TECHNOLOGY

Raise the pressure

Name _____   Date _____

▲ Draw your answers.

	What will happen to the balloon?
	What will happen to the balloon?
	What will happen to the syringe on the right?

DESIGN AND TECHNOLOGY

Moving on up, see page 32

Moving pictures

▲ Cut out the shapes and make the mechanisms.

Slide

cut on ✂ — — — — —

Lever

● punch holes   Use 🖈 paper fasteners to join the card.

You will need
masking tape.

**DESIGN AND
TECHNOLOGY**

Anyone can join

Name _____   Date _____

DESIGN AND
TECHNOLOGY

Sorting materials, see page 38; Sorting fabrics, see page 53

Sorting materials

Name _____ Date _____

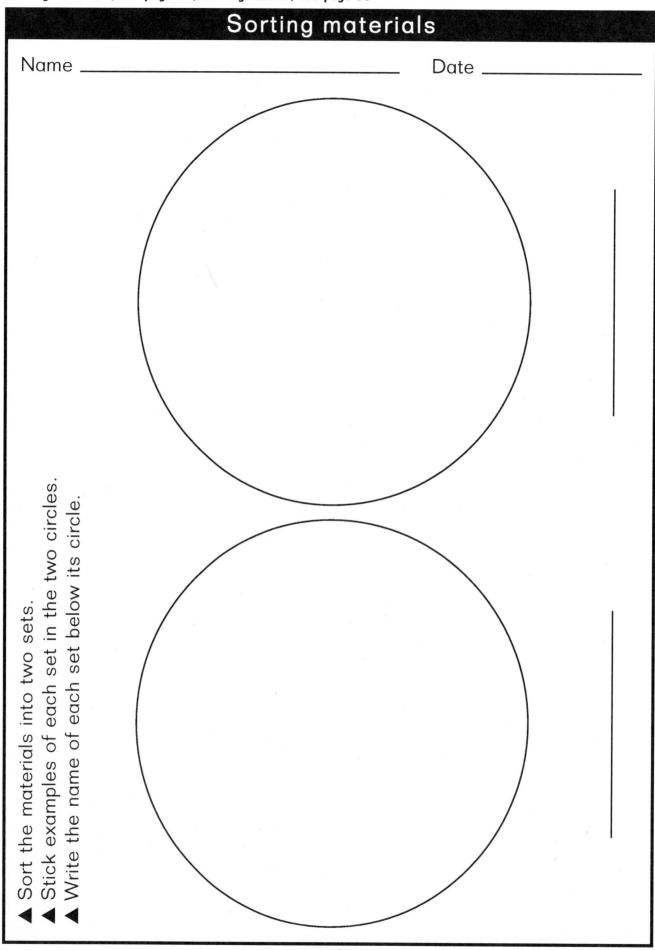

◀ Sort the materials into two sets.
◀ Stick examples of each set in the two circles.
◀ Write the name of each set below its circle.

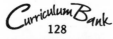

**DESIGN AND
TECHNOLOGY**

Looking at shapes, see page 39

What's in a shape?

Name _____ Date _____

▲ Draw the reclaimed materials you would use to make these models.

Object	Reclaimed materials

What else could you make?	What would you use?

DESIGN AND TECHNOLOGY

How strong is it? see page 44

Changing shape

Name _____ Date _____

Push	▲ Draw what happens to the box when it is pushed down.

Push	▲ Draw what happens to the box when it is pushed down.

DESIGN AND
TECHNOLOGY

Get it together! see page 50

Which fastening?

Name _____   Date _____

▲ Draw the right fastening in each circle.

cardigan

shoe

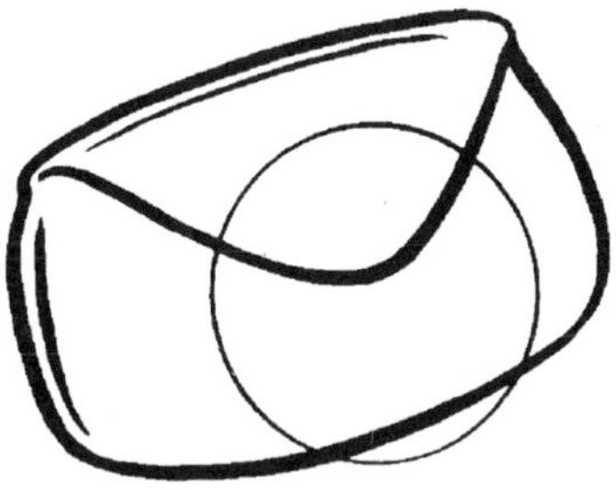

purse

trousers

football boot

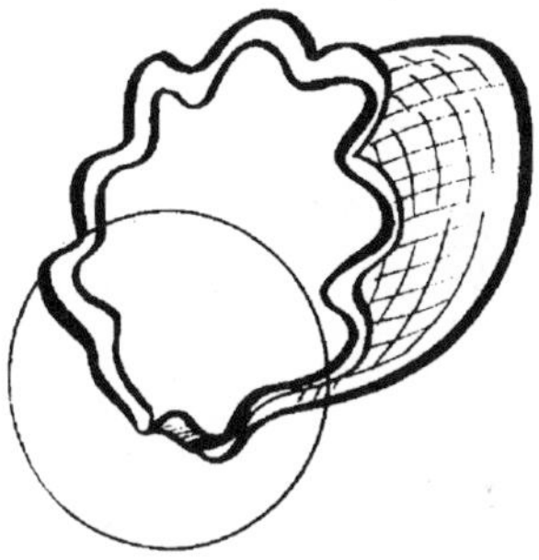

baby's bonnet

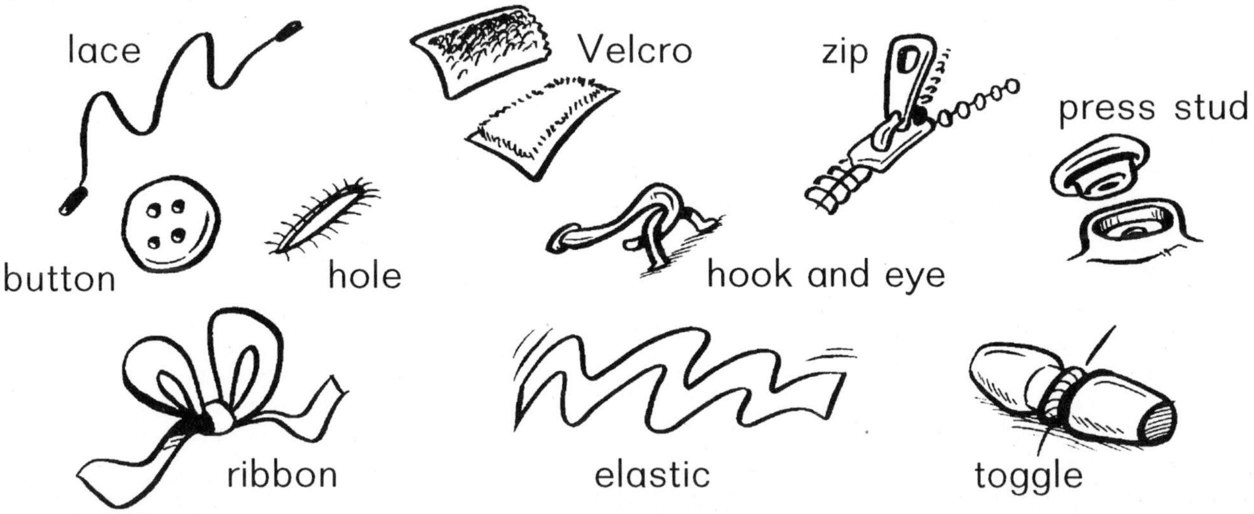

lace

Velcro

zip

press stud

button   hole   hook and eye

ribbon   elastic   toggle

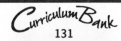

DESIGN AND
TECHNOLOGY

Photocopiables

Fabric fasteners, see page 55

Joining fabrics

Can you join your fabric using these different ways?

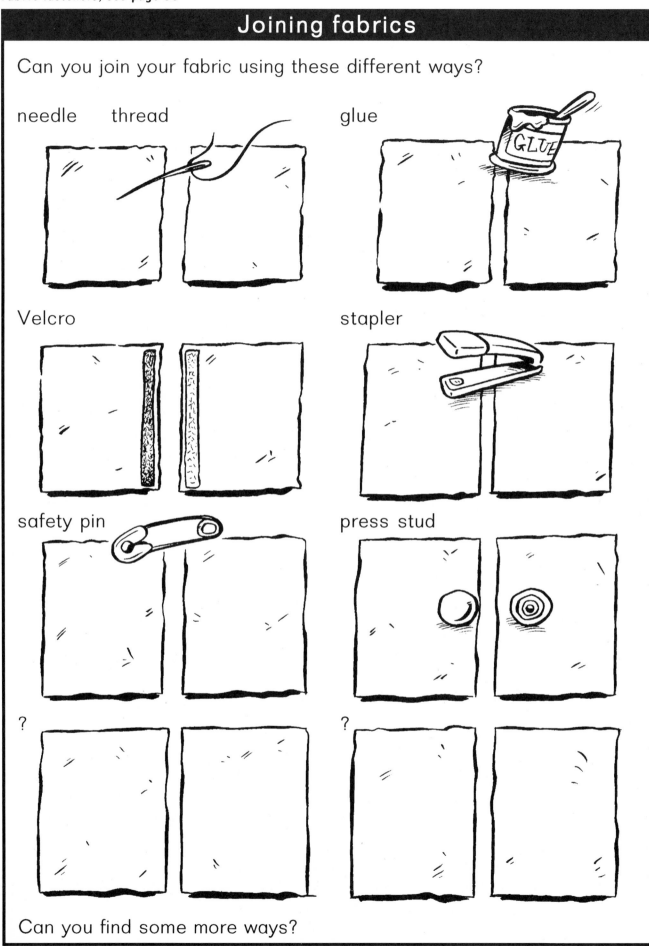

needle   thread   glue

Velcro   stapler

safety pin   press stud

?   ?

Can you find some more ways?

DESIGN AND
TECHNOLOGY

Using a pattern, see page 56

Using a pattern

▲ Cut out the patterns and use them to make clothing.

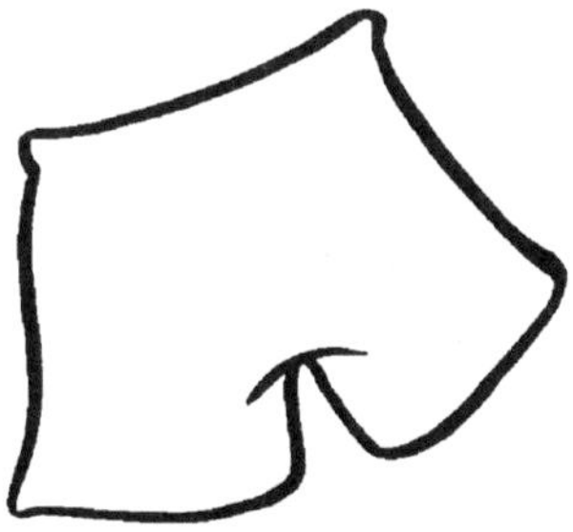

swimming trunks

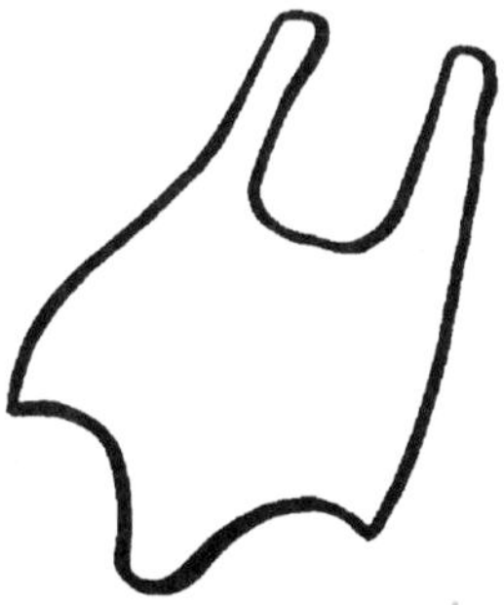

swimming costume

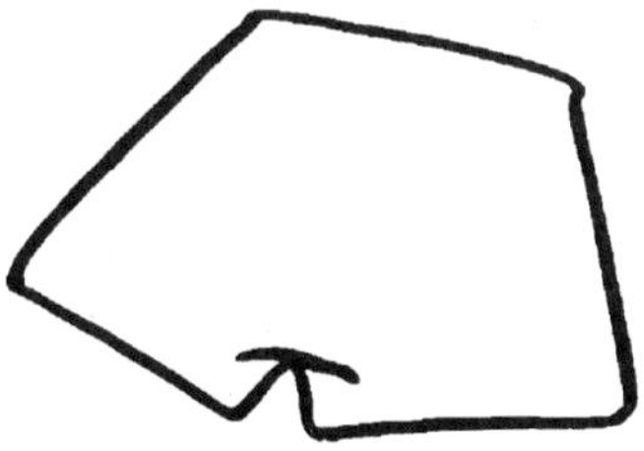

shorts

umbrella

boots

raincoat

winter coat

hat

mitten

jacket

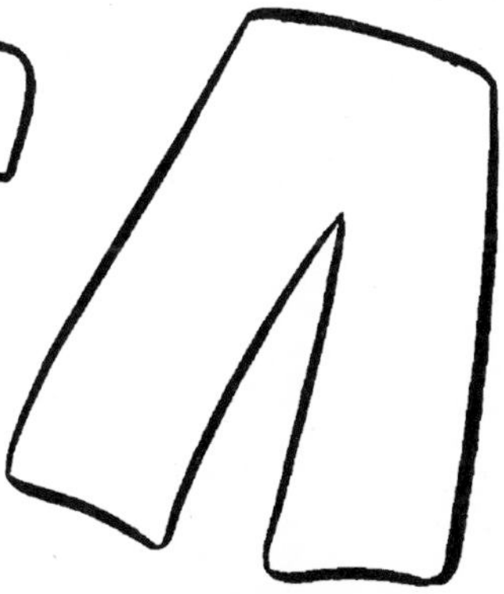

trousers

blouse

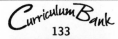

DESIGN AND
TECHNOLOGY

A special case, see page 58

Pattern for a comb/pencil case

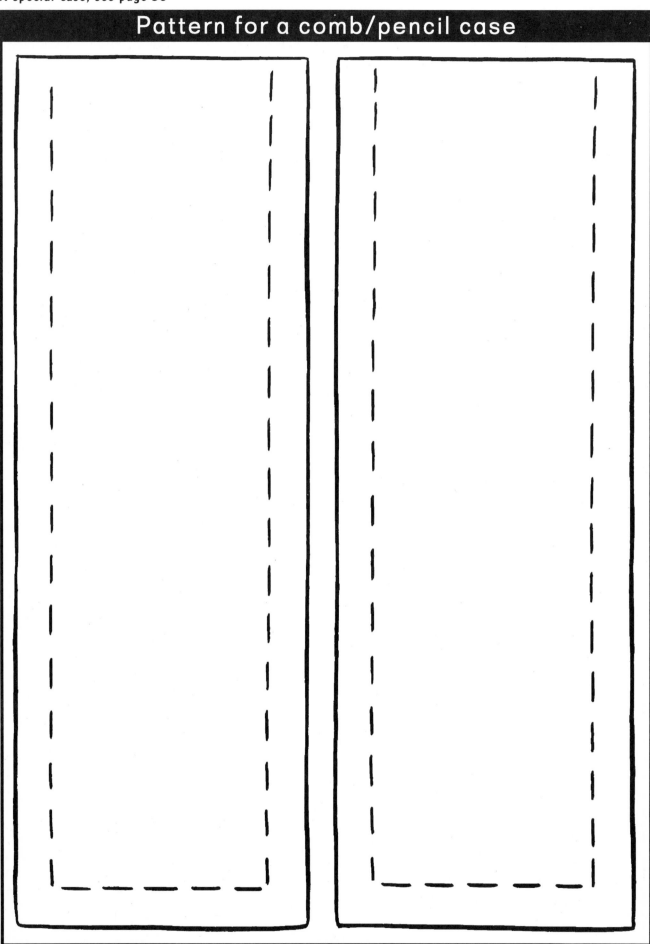

DESIGN AND TECHNOLOGY

How to stitch

How to hold the needle

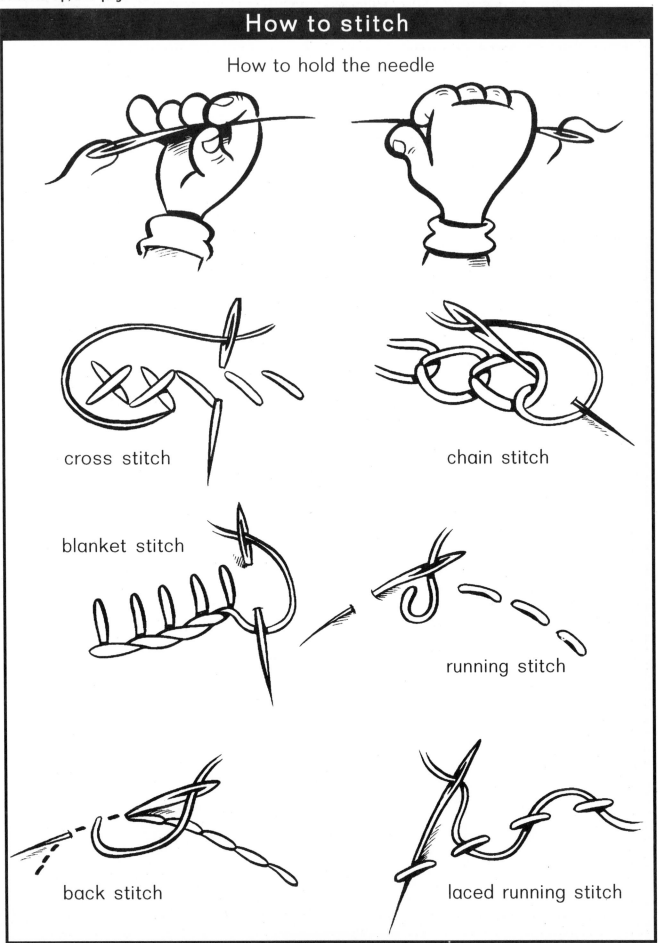

cross stitch

chain stitch

blanket stitch

running stitch

back stitch

laced running stitch

DESIGN AND TECHNOLOGY

Do it clean, see page 64

Working with food

hair tied back

sleeves back

no rings

clean hands

apron on

DESIGN AND
TECHNOLOGY

Tastes and textures, see page 65

Tastes and textures

Tastes

Food	Tastes like...	I like it	It's OK	I do not like it

Textures

Food	Feels like...	I like it	It's OK	I do not like it

DESIGN AND TECHNOLOGY

The naked lunch, see page 67

My sandwich

Name _____   Date _____

This is an example of what you might draw.

slice of brown
crunchy bread

crust (dark brown)

slice of brown
crunchy bread

filling (sticky red jam)

My sandwich is a △ triangle shape.

▲ Draw your sandwich here. Add writing to show what it is made of.

DESIGN AND
TECHNOLOGY

Sandwich fillings, see page 68

Our favourite fillings

Name _____   Date _____

▲ Fill in the names of the people you ask.
▲ Show what fillings they like, dislike or think are OK.

Name \ Filling				
Total Like OK Dislike				

like    OK 😐   dislike ☹

DESIGN AND TECHNOLOGY

Making buns, see page 70

Making buns

For a small group of children.
You need:

soft butter or margarine	1 egg	sugar	self-raising flour
measuring cup	**or** scales	plastic mixing bowl	small plastic container
fork	spoon	teaspoon	knife	sieve
paper cases	baking tray	cooling tray	oven gloves

1. Preheat oven to Gas Mark 5 (375°F/190°C).

2. Weigh out 55g butter or margarine and 55g sugar, and put them in the mixing bowl.

3. Cream together until almost white.

4. Crack the egg into a small plastic container, then add to the mixture.

5. Mix smoothly, with a circular movement.

6. Weigh out 55g flour and add to the mixture.

7. Mix until the mixture is creamy and smooth.

8. Put a large teaspoonful of the mixture into each paper case.

9. Put in the oven for about 15 minutes.

10. Let an adult take the buns out of the oven and put them on a cooling tray.

11. Do **not** touch until cool.

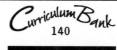

Wheel life, see page 74

A wheeled model

Name _____ Date _____

My workcard on how to make _____

You need these pieces

Next step

Next step

Next step

DESIGN AND TECHNOLOGY

Evaluating a construction kit, see page 75

Our kit

Name _____ Date _____

Name of kit: _____

▲ Circle what you think.

Appearance – what it looks like. Think about colour, shape, finish.	 1	2	3	 4
Safety – is it safe to use?	 1	2	3	 4
How does it fit together?	 1	2	3	 4
What mechanisms does it include?	a lot 1	2	3	not many 4
Overall	 1	2	3	 4

DESIGN AND TECHNOLOGY

Making a circuit, see page 85

Will it light?

Name _____   Date _____

✓ or X

☐

✓ or X

☐

✓ or X

☐

✓ or X

☐

▲ Draw your own circuits.

DESIGN AND TECHNOLOGY

A light switch, see page 87

Switch it on

Name _____   Date _____

battery and holder	bulb and holder
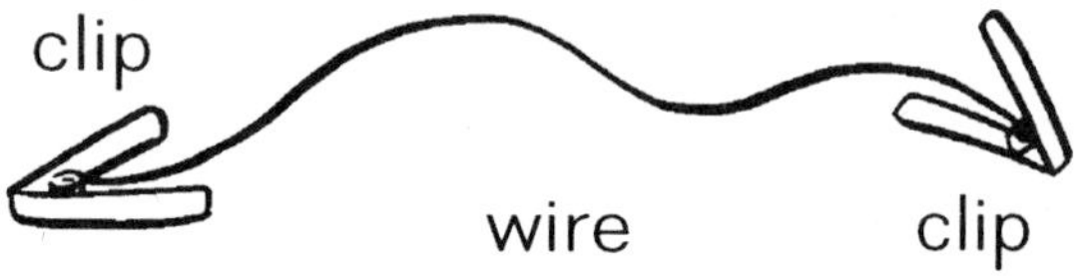 clip — wire — clip	switch
switch	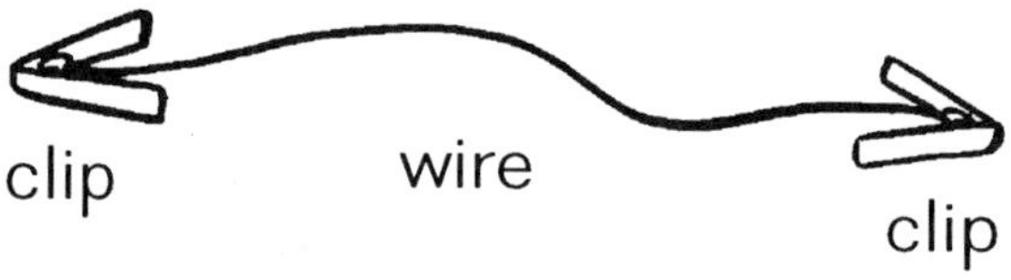 clip — wire — clip
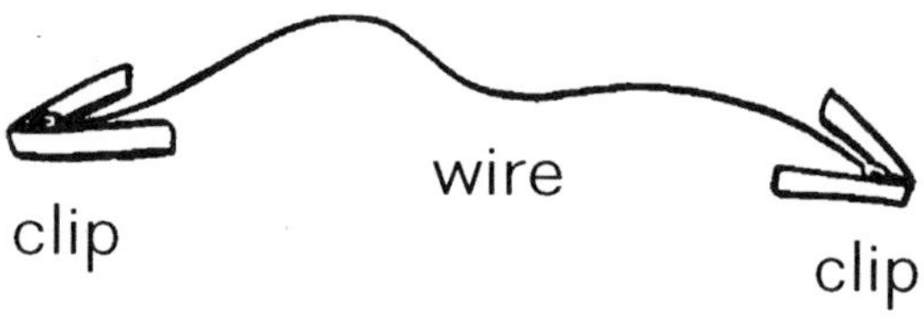 clip — wire — clip	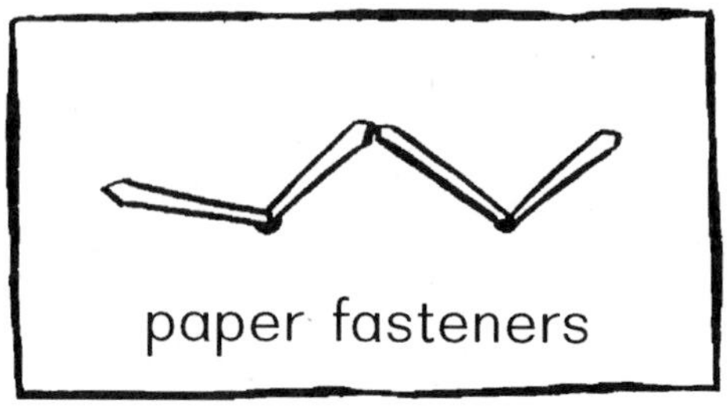 paper fasteners switch

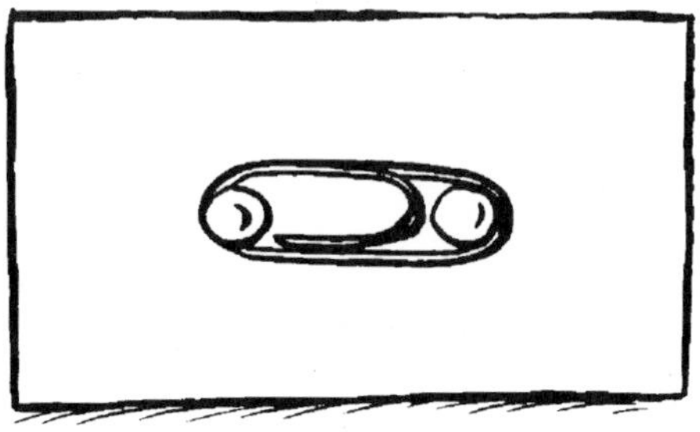

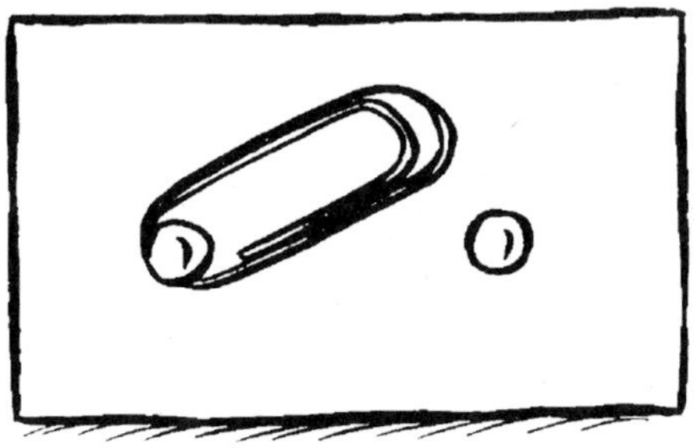

DESIGN AND
TECHNOLOGY

On and off, see page 88

Making a switch

Name _____   Date _____

Clip paper clip onto fastener.	tin foil kept on by drawing pin
Push in paper fasteners. card	soft wood block drawing pin
1. My switch (open)	**2.** My switch (open)
1. My switch (closed)	**2.** My switch (closed)

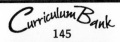
DESIGN AND TECHNOLOGY

A bright-nosed monster, see page 91

A bright-nosed monster

Name _____ Date _____

1 Put out all your equipment.

battery holder

battery

wires

bulb

holder

card

paper clips

paper fasteners

☐ ✓ when done

2 Make a circuit.

battery and holder

☐ ✓ when done

3 Make a switch.

paper clip

paper fastener

card

☐ ✓ when done

4 Put the switch into the circuit.

☐ ✓ when done

6 Cut the back off the box.

☐ ✓ when done

6 Make a small hole for the nose.

☐ ✓ when done

7 Put the circuit into the box.

push bulb through hole

switch

battery and holder

☐ ✓ when done

8 Create the monster's face.

☐ ✓ when done

DESIGN AND TECHNOLOGY

Drying out, see page 94

Investigating clay

Name _____ Date _____

What we want to find out:

What we need:

What we did:

What we found out:

DESIGN AND TECHNOLOGY

Useful things

Name _____ Date _____

What is it?

What is it used for?

Who uses it?

Why is it made from that material?

Why do you like it?

▲ Draw your item here.

DESIGN AND
TECHNOLOGY

Torn apart, see page 96

Papier mâché

Name _____ Date _____

Wet

Dry

DESIGN AND TECHNOLOGY

Shelter from the storm, see page 107

The shelter

Name _____ Date _____

Design and make a shelter for ....

My design:

▲ Try out ideas on the back of this sheet.

Materials I will use:

My shelter will need to be:

● _____

● _____

● _____

The village bus, see page 108

Our village bus

Every morning, very early, you can hear our village bus chugging along. It is very big and long, and it is yellow with white stripes along the side. The windows are wide, so everyone can see out. The village bus has to go down a dusty road which is very muddy when it rains. It picks up people at every stop. Everyone is going somewhere different. Some go to school, others go to town.

One Saturday, when the sky was blue, the village bus came to my stop. There were many people waiting to go to town, including my Koko (grandma). Everyone was dressed in their best clothes. The bus came. Everyone got on and it was very full. It started off to town, but suddenly the rain came. The clouds were big and black and the raindrops were enormous. The bus stopped. It was stuck in the mud. The driver, Old Modise, could not make it go.

People got out and pushed. My Koko shouted to them to push harder. Still the bus did not move. My Koko shouted again and waved her umbrella. Suddenly the bus moved out of the mud. Everyone cheered and cheered. They sang songs all the way to town. The sun came out, and soon the mud was drying up and the road was dusty again.

DESIGN AND TECHNOLOGY

Sweet delight, see page 110

Life is sweet

Name _____   Date _____

▲ Design and make sweets for _____

My sweets should be:

shape _____   colour _____

flavour _____

My design:

The sweets were _____

because _____

DESIGN AND TECHNOLOGY

Sweet recipe

What you need:

200 grams of **or** 2 cups of   a small
icing sugar   icing sugar   container of water

a dessertspoon   a fork   a mixing bowl

a paper plate   a doily   a cutter

Which will you choose?

flavourings      colourings

What you do
1. Put the icing sugar in the bowl.
2. Put in 1 spoonful of water.
3. Mix with a fork.
4. Add the colouring and flavouring.
5. Add **a little** more water and mix,
until the icing sugar is like a thick paste.
6. Roll out, cut and shape.
7. Put the sweets on a plate with a doily.

Living doll, see page 113

A moving puppet

Name _____   Date _____

My puppet is _____

I will make my puppet move like this:

I will use these materials:

_____ will look like this:

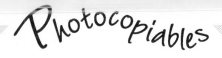

Present time, see page 114

Present time

Name _____   Date _____

I am going to make a _____

for _____

My gift will look like this:

▲ Add a label to tell about your gift.

_____ liked/did not like my gift because:

_____

Any changes?

DESIGN AND
TECHNOLOGY

Room for everyone, see page 115

Making a room

Names _____ and _____ Date _____

The room is the _____

Use the back of this sheet for first ideas.

Furniture we will make:

Wall coverings:

Floor coverings:

DESIGN AND TECHNOLOGY